# LIFE SKILLS WORKBOOK FOR CHILDREN WITH AUTISM AND SPECIAL NEEDS

*Susan Jules*

Get the Letter of Intent FOR FREE.

Sign up for the no-spam newsletter, and get the LETTER OF INTENT for free.

Details can be found at the end of the book.

The author and publisher have provided this e-book to you for your personal use only. You may not make this e-book publicly available in any way. Copyright infringement is against the law. If you believe the copy of this e-book you are reading infringes on the author's copyright, please notify us at diffnotless.com/piracy

# Table of Contents

## Chapter 6

### Social Skills Continued—Communication Games for Kids ...............77

### Chapter 7 ...................................................... 87

### Social Skills Continued—Problem-Solving Skills............................... 87

### Chapter 8
### Social Skills Continued—Accountability ........................................ 109

# Chapter 1

## Introduction

Children with special needs, such as autism, muscular dystrophy, Down syndrome, multiple sclerosis, chronic asthma, epilepsy, dyslexia, processing disorders, bipolar disorder, oppositional defiance disorder, and the like require the learning of life skills in order to promote independence at home, at school, and in public. Studies have indicated that early introductions to these skills, coupled with a block-by-block grooming approach greatly helps children with special needs acquire the skills needed for increasing their self-esteem, which invariably leads to added delight in all ramifications of life.

### A. Life Skills

Life skills sometimes denoted as autonomous or daily living skills, comprise self-care actions, cookery, cash management, shopping, space organization, and transportation. It is a fact that these skills are generally learned over time; however, the foundation for such learning begins from home, from a very young age, going on to mature even more throughout adolescence and adulthood.

A wide variety of life skills that apply to many ramifications of life must be taught to these children. Additionally, executive function or thinking skills such as planning, organizing, ranking, and decision-making related to each life skill being taught could serve as essential inclusions to the whole learning process.

Some life skills may include the following:

- Home living skills

- Self-determination/advocacy

- Community participation

- Personal finance

- Health and safety

- Career path and employment

- Transportation

- Peer-to-peer socialization and social communication

- Leisure/recreation

Right from 1943, when Leo Kanner first identified a cluster of children with an amazingly infrequent pattern of behavioral disorders to this day, when indicative and research apparatuses have become considerably more erudite in the detection of such disorders, society has gotten better at handling children with special needs. Educational approaches, being one of the earliest forms of interventions, have proven to be vital in this treatment, bringing about substantial improvements.

Regarding certain disorders such as autism, research has established that autism is not an exclusive and distinct condition as once assumed, but a continuum of disorders, with *classic autism* being the most critical, as most persons on the autism spectrum exhibit much milder symptoms. According to the U.S. Centers for Disease Control and Prevention, an estimated 1 in 152 individuals live with classic autism; with approximately 80 percent of those individuals being high functioning, possessing negligible impairments and no less than average intelligence and with males being affected seven times as much compared to females.

It is not uncommon to find children with special needs such as autism spectrum disorders (ASDs) in regular education classes. It is also common for teachers to be recurrently astonished by their display of behavior in class; nevertheless, these symptoms are time and again just minimal displays compared to the hardships that these children have to suffer.

One of the fundamental deficits of ASDs is a dearth in both nonverbal and verbal social dealings and communication; this is also accompanied by limitations in flexible and imaginative context-sensitive thinking. Young adults on the spectrum differ extensively in their mental capabilities and limitations, in addition to their personality and amiability, with most having intelligence that could be set at average or above.

In school, children on the spectrum have intense challenges in relating to their peers, irrespective of their level of intellectual ability. These challenges expose them to noteworthy possibilities for the formation of other behavioral and emotional challenges like anxiety.In addition, children on the spectrum find it increasingly difficult to learn how to nurture and manage more meaningful social relationships by merely observing other people or by taking part in different social activities. This is because they don't appear to have regulatory values as to how to secure the social information they need. All the same, they are very interested in learning, and various interventions conducted via research and outpatient clinic programs have indicated that children on the spectrum can certainly learn social communication and self-regulation skills. These kids are pleasurable to work with, typically ready to acquire new skills that aid them in fitting in, thanks to their having hardly any defenses that get in the way of learning, as they seldom hide their emotions or tell tales about their feelings.

## B. Prominent Approach to Social Skills Training

Typically, the idea is to ascertain a collective social state of affairs that can be deemed important and go on to impart each social etiquette as a chain of simple directions to follow. These methods have been known to help children and youngsters in grasping the concept of adaptation and fitting in based on the social context. Organizing social actions in relation to dire situations and attending to rules of propriety for each necessitates negligible contemplations of the perspectives of others; furthermore, it requires abstract thinking on the part of the children and youngsters on the spectrum.

Children's friendship training comes with distinct benefits, which this book covers in as many ways as time would allow; they include the following:

- It is well established that the involvement and participation of parents at various stages and phases is an integral part of the intermediation.

- An essential part of the whole management session is the giving and execution of homework assignments by the teachers and the youngsters, respectively.

- Some skills have been identified as great contributors to social competence in characteristically emerging neurotypical peers; these skills are employed and used in teaching group members.

- Another fact is that partaking in pleasant playdates between parents and their wards stimulates some of the best friendships. This is why parents and children are drafted alongside one another to work together to host get-togethers.

Other effective modules have been premeditated and adopted in a bid to address social issues specific to children with ASDs, some of which include the following:

- Pinpointing groups and peers that are most appropriate for the child. Once this is done, the child is further schooled on how to become a part of that group via basic conversation.

- Specifically coaching the child on how to manage and exit such a group if need be and in the event that being a part of such a group might be becoming toxic for their growth and development.

- Coaching the youngster on the subjects of teasing and embarrassing feedback from others and how to differentiate between constructive and destructive criticisms.

- Coaching the youngster on electronic communication, such as smartphone propriety and rules of text messaging.

## C. What This Book Seeks to Achieve

This book is intended to help parents, guardians, teachers, caregivers, and special educators who manage children on the spectrum to provide some semblance of regularity to their wards, encouraging them to improve their social behaviors towards others. Parents of tweens and teens on the spectrum often have to take on the advocacy role in the absence of services. Thus, parents may be interested in this book as it would be a useful resource for their child's teachers. This book helps teachers recognize the social problems of these adolescents and educates teachers on what they need to know about ASDs, discusses the advantages and disadvantages of different school options for these students, and gives them brief classroom interventions they can use to remedy social problems without further stigmatizing the teens. The book has two main purposes:

1.  To provide parents, guardians, and caregivers with a better grasp of the social defects present in children on the spectrum and those with special needs.

2.  To provide enough knowledge and guidance to parents and teacher on how to go about helping these children to improve their social, friendship, and life skills.

# Chapter 2

## Social Skills

### A. What Are Social Skills?

Social skills can be described as a set of skills needed for deployment in every day interactions and communications with others; these skills are techniques used in dealing with other people, which help in forming robust and constructive connections. Some of these vital skills include verbal and nonverbal communication, like speech, gesticulation, facial expression, and body language. Sturdy social skills can be developed in children from an early age; their manifestations are obvious, showing knowledge of how to conduct one's self in social circumstances and appreciating both written and inferred instructions when interacting with others.

Furthermore, good social skills let children relish improved relationships with their peers, and these virtues have been known to breed greater benefits far beyond social acceptance. Studies reveal that good social skills may aid in the reduction of stress-related difficulties in children who are exposed to daycare scenarios. Also, clear-cut communications and calm and respectful responses in children have all been pinned to the effects of possessing good social skills. Children with these skills also exhibit concerns for the feelings and interests of their peers, are quick and bold enough to take responsibility for their actions, are able to exhibit tremendous self-control, and display a great amount of assertion when the need arises.

The learning and adoption of various kinds of social skills in children are imperative, as they are the course to fashioning and maintaining relationships. Also, such skills are required for inspiring social proficiencies, lessening the odds for interactions that could be best described as undesirable. As they can be described as the building blocks for friendships, social skills put the child on the path of learning from their peers and learning how to be thoughtful of people they come in contact with in the future. Furthermore, social skills, having the potential to impact positively on life experiences, breed a sense of confidence and mastery in children over their lives and environment.

Typically, children tend to learn various social skills via experiences with peers, illustrations, and instructions from their parents and spending time with grown-ups.

## B. Why Are Social Skills Important?

Possessing sound social skills have been identified as essential in the empowerment of children in the formulation and maintenance of positive interactions with others; a lot of these skills are critical in assembling and supporting friendships. Characteristically, it is common for children to experience hiccups and setbacks in social interactions now and then, and they need to learn and apply appropriate approaches (like conflict resolution) when such complications in interactions come up. It is equally central for children to learn to display empathy, which is the act of putting oneself in someone else's shoes, recognizing and acknowledging their feelings; this gives room for responses that are rooted in understanding and care for the feelings of others.

As social skills have been identified to be an integral part of operating in society, grooming them, most especially in children prepares them for improved interactions in all facets of life. Assisting children in developing these vital skills would necessitate employing various sets of strategies in each period of development.

Naturally, some children, as is the case with a lot of grown-ups, are more obviously socially skillful compared to others. This category of people easily attract others and find that making friends comes easily to them. Social skills, like any other skill, can be taught and learned. What is essential, though, is that children can formulate evocative bonds with others, identify and interact with others suitably, and have the skills to adjust in tough situations.

It is important to begin by inspiring social skills in infants at a very early stage. Babies cannot say what exactly they need, at least not directly; this implies that the parent would need to give attention to actions and nonverbal prompts that the baby provides. Once these prompts are detected, it is expected that the parent or guardian would serve those needs appropriately.

Grown-ups often misconstrue the art of play in children; this they do by making assumptions that children play just to pass the time.

This assumption has been proven to be false. It is a fact that children advance most of their skills as they engage in play, and they use this exercise to explore the world around them. This is why playing should be encouraged amongst them as they will learn new skills while doing so. Parents also have vital roles to play during this exercise by offering their baby positive feedback. This improves the baby's self-confidence as they develop.

As the child advances in age, parents must openly discuss feelings with the toddler. This would help them in grasping and interpreting their feelings and that of others. By conversing about how they feel, parents open the door for the child to learn words concomitant with those feelings, which can later be used in their conversations, as they try to verbally express their feelings. This action helps the child switch to talking about feelings as a replacement for acting out those frustrations.

| As a general rule, children are expected to have developed definite social skills and social cues by the following ages: | |
|---|---|
| **Ages two to three years** | ▪ Can try to seek attention from others<br><br>▪ Can initiate social contact with others (verbally and physically)<br><br>▪ Can look at a person who is talking<br><br>▪ Can take turns talking<br><br>▪ Can laugh at inane objects and events |
| **Ages three to four years** | ▪ Can take turns while playing games<br><br>▪ Can play with a doll or stuffed animals<br><br>▪ Can begin verbal communication with definite words. |
| **Ages four to five years** | ▪ Can display more cooperation with children<br><br>▪ Can use direct requests<br><br>▪ Can chat and indulge in pretend play |
| **Ages five to six years** | ▪ Can gratify their friends<br>▪ Can say "I'm sorry," "Please," and "Thank you"<br>▪ Can be more strategic in negotiating<br>▪ Can play competitive games<br>▪ Can grasp fair play and good sportsmanship |

## C. Why Learning Social Skills Can Be Challenging

Many reasons abound as to why a child could have a dearth of social skills. It may be due to the absence of knowledge, such as the failure to gain new skills, or due to deficit incompetency. At other times, the child may know how to execute the social skill but may find it hard to do so due to insufficient practice or scanty feedback. Furthermore, internal or external factors exist that can inhibit individual performances when it comes to social skills, things such as anxiety or chaotic surroundings. Also, children diagnosed with various neurotypical ailments, such as ASD, pervasive developmental disorder, Asperger's, and the like all have troubles with social skills.

**Below are five common types of social skills deficits:**

*Basic communication skills.*

Basic communication skills comprise the skill of listening, following instructions, and refraining from speaking. Good listening skills entail concentration abilities and paying no attention to distractions. Furthermore, they are validated by showing attention through smiling, nodding, and giving feedback on what has been said or deliberated. Good listening skills also consist of the aptitude to revert to past comments, for instance, linking a current statement to a previous one or interrogation about possible, future ideas, actions, and dealings. Basic communication skills take account of body language and behaviors, such as eye contact, physical stillness, and emotional attentiveness while the other person is talking.

*Interpersonal skills.*

Interpersonal skills comprise the knacks of sharing, linking activities, probing for permission, and waiting turns. For children who have social skill deficiencies, such as children with ASD or other special needs, they may find asking accurate and concise questions quite frustrating. Furthermore, being unable to ask simple questions from blockades makes getting information difficult. Being unable to ask simple questions can give a false impression of the child appearing not to be fair-minded and even be antisocial. Having poor social skills may trigger the asking of closed questions as that type of question prompts brief and well-ordered responses. Grown-ups with imperfect social skills may find it difficult to grasp proper etiquette in dissimilar social contexts and situations.

*Empathy and Relationship Skills.*

These skills encapsulate the ability of an individual to comprehend the experience of other people and do this from their perspective. This comprises paying careful attention to what others have to say and then communicating your appreciation of the message back to them.

Typically, empathy and relationship skills involve two main modules:

- A pledge to plunge oneself in the viewpoint of another in order to grasp the situation from their standpoint, and

- Sharing such a grasp with the other person, so that they know how well you understand their situation.

14

Certain cognitive conditions, such as ASD alongside other behavioral and mental health conditions have been known to inhibit the ability to feel empathy and bond with others. It is characteristic of those who suffer from severe social anxiety or high levels of self-consciousness to become excessively or abysmally focused on someone else. This implies that some individuals with anxiety are desperate to please others and avoid clashes; this is so that they can pay close attention to what others say or always offer to help or do favors. On the other hand, some individuals feel flabbergasted by their social environment to the point of shutting down when they are around other people.

### Problem-solving skills.

Problem-solving skills comprise querying for help, saying sorry to others, determining what to do, and accepting consequences. For some children, identifying the core causes of problems can be very challenging; this implies that they cannot fully grasp possible solutions or approaches. Typically, children who find solving problems hard may be melancholically shy or clinically reclusive. Additionally, they tend to avoid problems altogether, as it makes them feel uncomfortable. This evasion of problems could further lead to poor formation of conflict resolution skills in the future. Again, some children constantly struggle when it comes to dealing with teasing appropriately; others might struggle with accepting losses in games and competition.

### Accountability.

Accountability involves accepting corrections and criticisms from others without feeling emotionally hurt, keeping to one's words, promises and vow, keeping faith with responsibility and seeing them to their expected end, and so on. A deficit in this skill can lead to struggles with accommodating liabilities for problems or handling constructive feedback. Naturally, accountability is closely associated with reliability and maturity.

Promising to do a thing and then failing to do it could be attributed to some legitimate excuses, but an obvious lack of accountability may show gross unreliability and immaturity. Furthermore, accountability has been proven to be a vital part of conflict management;this is because identifying mistakes are an exceptional way to point out peacemaking and a willing attitude.

## D. Identifying Social Skills in Your Child

Typically, children with special needs, such as ASD, foundationally have challenges with the formulation and demonstration of social skills; however, here are a few points to note in order to ascertain if a child has difficulties with social skills.

Below are a few observations for determining if a child has challenges with their social skills. Please tick the appropriate option for each column.

| Challenges | Yes | No | Not sure |
|---|---|---|---|
| <ul><li>Uses transitory eye contact, doesn't regularly use eye contact, or watches fixedly</li><li>Unable to take turns while talking to others</li><li>Struggles with using suitable body language</li><li>Doesn't employ polite forms of communication</li><li>Incapable of initiating and ending conversations</li><li>Interjects others often</li><li>Incapable of maintaining a topic of conversation and offers unrelated comments throughout a chat</li><li>Talks "at you" in a conversation instead of talking "with" you</li><li>Unable to ask appropriate questions</li><li>Repeats info in conversation and is inclined to talk about topics of their interest</li><li>Displays little or no interest in what the others have to say</li><li>Incapable of understanding jokes and language, like sarcasm, idioms, and nonliteral information</li><li>Construes what is said in a very literal way</li><li>Dialogues with infrequent speed, stress, rhythm, intonation, pitch, and/or tone of voice</li><li>Incapable of grasping diverse tones of voice or recognizing facial cues</li><li>Doesn't ask for elucidation when confused</li><li>Finds it hard to react suitably when asked to change actions</li><li>Divulges personal info to strangers excessively</li><li>Seems oblivious of others; fails to recognize feelings based on verbal and nonverbal cues of others</li><li>Incapable of suitably responding to teasing, anger, failure, and disappointment</li></ul> | | | |

| | | | |
|---|---|---|---|
| • Incapable of suitably adjusting or modifying their language according to the situation<br>• Lacks empathy<br>• Lacks imagination<br>• Appears self-centered<br>• Unable to grasp the consequences of actions | | | |

Do you have any observations that you feel should be included? Write them down here:

_____

_____

_____

_____

List some of the behaviors you have observed under the following categories:

| | |
|---|---|
| Behavioral (such as refusing to go to school) | _____<br><br>_____ |
| Articulatory (such as clarity and appropriateness of speech) | _____<br><br>_____ |
| Voice (such as intonation, hue, pitch) | _____<br><br>_____ |
| Self-regulatory (such as keeping calm, changing emotions) | _____<br><br>_____ |
| Sensory processing (such as keeping focus) | _____<br><br>_____ |
| Completing tasks (such as homework and household chores) | _____<br><br>_____ |

# Chapter 3

## Social Skills Continued—Basic Communication Skills

### A. Teaching About Respecting Spaces

| Category of activity | Illustrative/role-playing |
|---|---|
| Objective | The idea behind this lesson is to point out to the child that other people cherish their personal spaces and therefore must be respected, be it when talking to them, relating, or forming a queue. Respecting other people's space would invariably mean they would reciprocate the gesture whenever they can. |
| Items to use | <ul><li>A toy, an action figure, or a doll will do</li><li>A chair</li></ul> |

**The Lesson**

- Begin by explaining the following to the child:

  o "A secret social rule when talking to others is to stand or sit an acceptable distance away from the other person.

  o Sitting or standing too close is called *invading their space.*

- Stand at least an arm's length away when talking with another person.

- Remember not to get too close, except when you are talking with your mom or dad.

- Respect other children's spaces when playing with them."

- Get a child to sit on the chair

- Ask the child to go close to the child who is seated; once they get too close, make them stop, and point out that such a distance is inappropriate.

- Ask the child to move back a bit; once the appropriate distance is reached, stop the child, and point out this distance as right.

- Get a child to play with the toy on the floor.

- Ask the other child to approach the child on the floor, asking if they too can play with the toy.

- Once the child gets too close, make them stop and point out that such a distance is inappropriate.

- Ask the child to move back a bit; once the appropriate distance is reached, stop the child, and point out this distance as right.

- Repeat with other scenarios at your disposal, such as when standing in line or when saying hello to others.

> Take note of the various responses of the child at each stage and with each instruction.

**Important notes:**

_____

_____

_____

_____

_____

_____

_____

_____

_____

_____

# B. Teaching About Listening (One)

| Category of activity | Illustrative/role-playing |
|---|---|
| Objective | The idea behind this lesson is to point out to the child that other people like it when we listen to what it is they are saying. Respecting other people enough to listen to what they have to say and respond in such a manner that convinces them of our undivided attention. |
| Items to use | ▪ A toy, an action figure, or a doll will do<br>▪ Two chairs |

21

**The Lesson**

- Begin by explaining the following to the child:

  - "It is important for you to be a good listener when someone else is talking. This means your mind and your body must be involved.

  - Here are a few things to do when listening to others:

    - Make eye contact.

    - Steady and still hands and feet.

    - Keep quiet. It is rude to talk while other people are talking."

- Ask the child to sit. You too should sit facing the child.

- Take the toy and begin to talk about the toy.Say, "This is Bonnie the Doll... she is pretty..." and so on.

- Once the child breaks eye contact for an extended period, pause and remind them to keep it fixed on you.

- Encourage the child to be quiet and steady; use a soft tone to remind them to stay still.

- Once you are done, give the toy to the child, and ask them to say a few words about the toy.

- Make sure you respect the rules of listening as the child speaks.

- Repeat with other scenarios at your disposal.

Take note of the various responses of the child at each stage and with each instruction.

Important notes:

_____

_____

_____

_____

_____

_____

_____

_____

## C. Teaching About Listening (Two)

| Category of activity | Illustrative/role-playing |
|---|---|
| Objective | The idea behind this lesson is to point out to the child that an effective conversation involves listening and responding to what was said.<br><br>If responses are far off from the topic being discussed, this implies that listening isn't good enough and might ruin the conversation. |
| Items to use | ▪ A toy, an action figure, or a doll will do.<br>▪ Two chairs |

**The Lesson**

- Begin by explaining the following to the child:

    o "It is important for you to listen carefully when someone else is talking.

    o Remember to do the following:

        ▪ Make eye contact.

        ▪ Steady and still hands and feet.

        ▪ Keep quiet. It is rude to talk while other people are talking.

        ▪ Pay attention, and ask questions where you do not understand."

- Ask the child to sit. You too should sit facing the child

- Take the toy, and begin to talk about the toy.Say, "This is Tommy the Wolf... he is strong..." and so on.

- Once the child breaks eye contact for an extended period, pause and remind them to keep it fixed on you.

- Encourage the child to be quiet and steady; use a soft tone to remind them to stay still.

- Once you are done, ask the child if they have any questions to ask.

- Ask the child a few questions about the toy to gauge their level of attentiveness to your story.

- Give the toy to the child, and ask them to say a few words about the toy.

- Make sure you respect the rules of listening as the child speaks.

- Repeat with other scenarios at your disposal.

Take note of the various responses of the child at each stage and with each instruction.

Important notes:

_____

_____

_____

_____

_____

_____

_____

_____

# D. Teaching About Interrupting Others

| Category of activity | Illustrative/role-playing |
|---|---|
| Objective | The idea behind this lesson is to point out to the child that it is inappropriate for them to interrupt others when they are talking to them or others.<br><br>As much as the child might need the attention of another person, there are polite ways to go about getting it. Interrupting others can make one look selfish and inconsiderate. |
| Items to use | ▪ A toy, an action figure, or a doll will do.<br>▪ Two chairs |

**The Lesson**

- Begin by explaining the following to the child:

  o "Interrupting others in the middle of what they are saying or doing is considered rude and must be avoided. Sometimes though, it is OK to interrupt, like in the following instances:

    ▪ You need information, assistance, or guidance.

    ▪ In case of emergency.

    ▪ If you need something urgently.

  o You can walk up to the person, and then wait for them to pause in their conversation or activity.

26

- o You can say, "*Excuse* me..." before asking for what you need.

- o Once done, wait for their response.

- o As soon as they respond to your request, say, "thank you" before leaving."

- Ask two children to sit on the chairs.

- Instruct one of them to pick up the toy and speak to the other about it.

- You then approach the child talking and wait for a pause in the conversation before saying, "Excuse me, can I take a look at your doll?"

- Once done, pass the toy back to the child and say, "thank you" before walking away.

- Switch places with one of the children, and encourage them to do what they saw you do earlier.

- Repeat with other scenarios at your disposal.

**Take note of the various responses of the child at each stage and with each instruction.**

**Important notes:**

_____

_____

_____

_____

_____

_____

_____

_____

_____

# E. Teaching About Greeting Others

| Category of activity | Illustrative/role-playing |
|---|---|
| Objective | The idea behind this lesson is to point out to the child that it is important to greet people either by saying, "Hi" or using other forms of pleasantries. Greetings are a way of easily connecting with others once we meet, and they show we care about them to enquire about their day. |
| Items to use | ▪ None |

**The Lesson**

- Begin by explaining the following to the child:

28

o "It is polite to say, "Hi" or some other form of greeting when you see someone you know."

- The first time you see someone in the morning, say, "Good morning."

- When you meet someone on the way, say, "Hi."

- When you see someone is leaving for the day, say, "Bye," "Goodbye," or "See you later.""

- Stage a role-play scenario. Instruct the child to stay a few feet away from you.

- Approach the child and say, "Good morning. How are you today?" Allow the child to respond while gently correcting them where necessary.

- Do a reverse act, where the child approaches you to exchange pleasantries.

- Repeat with other scenarios at your disposal.

Take note of the various responses of the child at each stage and with each instruction.

Important notes:

_____

_____

_____

_____

_____

_____

_____

_____

## F. Teaching About Beginning and Maintaining Conversations

| Category of activity | Illustrative/role-playing |
|---|---|
| Objective | The idea behind this lesson is to point out to the child that starting a conversation isn't rocket science; it is something that can be learned and perfected with time.<br>Being a good conversationalist takes regular practice, constant adjustments, and delight. |
| Items to use | ▪ A toy, a doll, or an action figure would do.<br>▪ Two chairs |

**The Lesson**

- Begin by explaining the following to the child:

o "Starting a conversation is easy and can be done in a number of ways. One way is to talk about something that is on in the present moment.

- When you meet a person for the first time during the day, greet them.

- Ask a question about what they are doing.

  i. *What are you reading?*

  ii. *What are you watching?*

  iii. *What are you playing with?*

- Ask follow-up questions related to the activity, using *Who, What, Where, Why,* and *How.*"

- Stage a role-play scenario. Instruct one child to sit on the chair and play with a toy.

- Approach the child who is sitting, and say, "Good morning. How are you today? May I sit beside you?" Allow a response from the child who is seated while gently correcting them where necessary.

- Inquire about what the child is doing, "What are you doing? Your doll is lovely. What's its name?

- Once done, do a reversal, where the child initiates and sustains the conversation following your initial illustrations.

- Repeat with other scenarios at your disposal.

- You can encourage a role-play in which the conversation is triggered by questions about the past; such as, "How did your day at school go today?" or "Tell me about your birthday party last weekend."

Take note of the various responses of the child at each stage and with each instruction.

Important notes:

_____

_____

_____

_____

_____

_____

_____

# G. Teaching About Ending Conversations

| Category of activity | Illustrative/role-playing |
|---|---|
| Objective | The idea behind this lesson is to point out to the child that ending a conversation is possible and should be considered sometimes.<br><br>Being a good conversationalist takes regular practice, constant adjustments, and delight. Ending a conversation is also a skill they ought to master to save time. |
| Items to use | • A toy, a doll, or an action figure would do.<br>• Two chairs |

**The Lesson**

- Begin by explaining the following to the child:

    o "Sometimes, it is normal to want to end a conversation with another person. Some reasons for this may include:

        ▪ You may have gotten bored.

        ▪ You may need to leave.

        ▪ You may want to talk about or do something else entirely.

    o Make up your mind if ending the conversation is what you want.

    o Wait until you have asked at least one question, and the person has responded to it.

- o   Say, "It was nice talking with you, but I have to go right now. See you later.""

- Stage a role-play scenario. Instruct one child to sit on the chair and play with a toy.

- Approach the child who is sitting, and say, "Good morning. How are you today? May I sit beside you?" Allow a response from the child who is seated while gently correcting them where necessary.

- Once you have determined that the child has responded to at least one of your questions, say, "It was nice talking with you, but I have to go right now. See you later." Then stand up and leave.

- Once done, do a reversal, where the child initiates, sustains, and ends the conversation by following your initial illustrations.

- Repeat with other scenarios at your disposal.

Take note of the various responses of the child at each stage and with each instruction.

Important notes:

_____

_____

_____

_____

_____

_____

_____

_____

## H. Teaching About Introducing Self to Others

| Category of activity | Illustrative/role-playing |
|---|---|
| Objective | The idea behind this lesson is to point out to the child that self-introduction is a chance to tell others a little about oneself. Introducing oneself to others can serve as a conversation starter and also help with adequate bonding with peers. |
| Items to use | ▪ A toy, a doll, or an action figure would do.<br>▪ Two chairs |

### The Lesson

• Begin by explaining the following to the child:

o   *"Whenever* you meet a person whom you haven't met before, you would have to introduce yourself to that person.

o   Always remember that if the other person is talking, you ought to wait for a pause in the conversation before saying anything.

o   Walk up to the person, stand an arm's length away, and make good eye contact.

o   Once you have their attention, say, *"Hi. My name is* _____. *What's your name?"* Then wait for their

response.

o   Then say, *"It's nice to meet you,* _____ " and shake hands."

• Stage a role-play scenario. Instruct one child to sit on the chair and play with a toy.

• Approach the child who is sitting, and say, "Hi. My name is _____. What's your name?" Allow a response from the sitting child while gently correcting them where necessary.

• Once the child replies with their name, say, "It's nice to meet you, _____." Go ahead and extend your arm for a handshake.

• Once done, do a reversal, where the child initiates, sustains, and ends the self-introduction following your initial illustrations.

- Repeat with other scenarios at your disposal, such as doing a self-introduction to more than one person at a time or doing so to a much older person, male and female, and so on.

**Take note of the various responses of the child at each stage and with each instruction.**

**Important notes:**

_____

_____

_____

_____

_____

_____

_____

_____

# I. Teaching About Talking Briefly

| Category of activity | Illustrative/role-playing |
|---|---|
| Objective | The idea behind this lesson is to point out to the child that not every conversation needs to be sustained; they have to look out for signs of whether or not the other person is enjoying the conversation.<br><br>A good conversationalist must know when to stop talking; they must learn to follow through with other listeners and gauge their level of engagement. It is all right to end a conversation on account of the other person being bored and uninterested. |
| Items to use | ▪ A toy, a doll, or an action figure would do.<br>▪ Two chairs |

## The Lesson

- Begin by explaining the following to the child:

    o "When speaking to another person, always look for signs that show that the other person is still interested in what you are talking about.

    o If the other person appears bored or uninterested, ask, *"Do you want to hear more?""*

    o If the other person no longer wants to hear more, then stop talking.

    o You can ask, *"What do you want to talk about now?"* Allow the other person to respond.

- Stage a role-play scenario. Instruct one child to sit on the chair.

- Approach the child, who is sitting, with a toy in your hand and say, *"Hi _____. Let me tell you about my doll over here."*

- Begin to talk about the doll—its name, how old it is, your favorite way of dressing it, and so on.

- Once you notice the child is losing interest, ask, *"Do you want to hear more?"* Wait for the other child to respond.

- Go on to ask, *"All right. What do you want us to talk about?"* the response of the child is not in the affirmative.

- Once done, do a reversal, where the child initiates, sustains, and ends the conversation by following your initial illustrations.

- Repeat with other scenarios at your disposal, such as talking about past activities.

---

**Take note of the various responses of the child at each stage and with each instruction.**

**Important notes:**

_____

_____

_____

_____

_____

_____

_____

_____

## J. Teaching About Asking for Clarifications While Talking

| Category of activity | Illustrative/role-playing |
|---|---|
| Objective | The main objective of this lesson is to point out to the child that the idea behind talking is to get clear-cut conversation at all times. If what is being discussed leads to further confusion, then the aim of the conversation is defeated. A good conversationalist must know when to ask for clarification in areas of the conversation where they are not quite clear. |
| Items to use | ▪ A toy, a doll, or an action figure would do. ▪ Two chairs |

**The Lesson**

- Begin by explaining the following to the child:

  o "When speaking to another person, always listen attentively to what is being said to avoid misconstruing what was said.

  o If you miss a point or aren't clear with a word or sentence, ask politely that the other person repeats the sentence or sheds more light on what was said. Say, *"Pardon me, but I didn't get what you just said."*

  o If the other person isn't speaking loud enough for you to hear, say, *"Pardon me _____. Can you speak a little louder. I really can't hear you.""*

- Stage a role-play scenario. Instruct one child to sit on the chair with a toy in their hand.

- Sit beside the child and ask, *"Hey, _____. Can you tell me a little about your doll?"*

- Listen attentively to each word.

- Occasionally ask, "Pardon me _____, *but can you speak up a little louder?"* *"What did you say the doll's name is again?"* *"Please can you say that again? I didn't get you the first time."* Once these questions are answered, respond with a *"thank you."*

- Allow the child to go on for a few minutes before politely ending the conversation and walking away.

- Once done, do a reversal, where the child initiates, sustains, and ends the conversation by following your initial illustrations.

- Repeat with other scenarios at your disposal, such as talking about past activities.

Take note of the various responses of the child at each stage and with each instruction.

**Important notes:**

_____

_____

_____

_____

_____

_____

_____

_____

# Chapter 4

## Social Skills Continued—Interpersonal Skills

### A. Teaching About Asking Another to Play

| Category of activity | Illustrative/role-playing |
|---|---|
| Objective | The idea behind this lesson is to point out to the child that asking another person to play is both courteous and helpful in forming newer friendships. Playing with others will open up a child to various levels of interpersonal relations with other children and begin the process of bonding with individuals and eventually with peers. |
| Items to use | ▪ A collection of toys<br>▪ A play mat |

**The Lesson**

- Begin by explaining the following to the child:

  o "When on a playground, a lot of other children want to play with you, but you have to ask them first.

  o Go pick up your favorite toy from the pile—the one you wish to share with your new friend.

  o Approach the other child. Wait for them to look directly at you.

- o Smile and say, *"Hi. My name is _____. Do you want to play?""*

- Stage a role-play scenario. Instruct one child to sit on the play mat with a toy.

- Approach the child, who is sitting, with a toy in your hand and say, *"Hi. My name is_____. Do you want to play?"*

- If the child on the play mat responds in the affirmative, sit and play with them.

- If the child says, *"I'm sorry, but I can't play with you right now,"* respond with, *"That's OK. Maybe later."* Then walk away with a smile.

- Once done, do a reversal, where the child initiates, sustains, and ends the conversation by following your initial illustrations.

- Repeat with other scenarios at your disposal, such as talking about past activities.

Take note of the various responses of the child at each stage and with each instruction.

Important notes:

_____

_____

_____

_____

_____

_____

_____

_____

## B. Teaching About Joining Others in Play

| Category of activity | Illustrative/role-playing |
|---|---|
| Objective | The idea behind this lesson is to point out to the child that joining others in play is both courteous and helpful in forming newer friendships. <br> Playing with others helps the child develop interpersonal skills that foster bonding with individuals and eventually with peers. |
| Items to use | ▪ A collection of toys <br> ▪ A play mat |

## The Lesson

- Begin by explaining the following to the child:

o "When on a playground, a lot of other children want to play with you; but you have to ask them first.

o Go pick up your favorite toy from the pile—the one you wish to share with your new friends.

o Approach the other children. Wait for them to look directly at you.

o Smile and say, *"Hi. My name is* _____. *Can I join in and play?""*

- Stage a role-play scenario. Instruct a group of children to sit and play on the play mat with various toys.

- Approach the children sitting on the play mat with a toy in your hand and say, *"Hi. My name is*_____. *Can I join in and play?"*

- If one of the children on the play mat responds in the affirmative, sit and play with them.

- Once done, do a reversal, where the child initiates, sustains, and ends the conversation by following your initial illustrations.

- Repeat with other scenarios at your disposal, such as talking about past activities.

**Take note of the various responses of the child at each stage and with each instruction.**

**Important notes:**

_____

_____

_____

_____

_____

_____

_____

_____

# C. Teaching About Sharing

| Category of activity | Illustrative/role-playing |
|---|---|
| Objective | The idea behind this lesson is to point out to the child that sharing is one way to be both courteous and helpful in forming newer friendships.<br>Being open to sharing what one has with others triggers a sense of selflessness and promotes potential cohesion between individuals and eventually between peers. |
| Items to use | ▪ A collection of toys<br>▪ A play mat |

## The Lesson

- Begin by explaining the following to the child:

- o "When on a playground, you can easily win a friend by offering to share one of your favorite toys. There are many reasons to share:

  - It will make the person you are sharing with happy.

  - It shows the person that you like them.

  - You win friends: Friends share with other friends.

- o Go pick up your favorite toy from the pile—the one you wish to share with your new friend.

- o Approach the other child. Wait for them to look directly at you.

- o Smile and say, *"Hi. My name is _____. Would you like to share my favorite toy?""*

- Stage a role-play scenario. Instruct a child to sit on the play mat.

- Approach the children sitting on the play mat with a toy in your hand and say, *"Hi. My name is_____. Would you like to share my favorite toy?"*

- If one of the children on the play mat responds in the affirmative, sit and play with them.

- Repeat with other scenarios at your disposal.

> Take note of the various responses of the child at each stage and with each instruction.

**Important notes:**

_____

_____

_____

_____

_____

_____

_____

_____

_____

# D. Teaching About Compromising

| Category of activity | Illustrative/role-playing |
|---|---|
| Objective | The idea behind this lesson is to point out to the child that part of what makes friendship thrive is through the art of compromise.<br>Having a singular opinion or always wanting to have one's way can hurt any friendship. It is always better to consider the needs of the other person. This will help them see that they too are stakeholders in the ongoing friendship. |
| Items to use | A collection of toys |

**The Lesson**

- Begin by explaining the following to the child:

  o "When on a playground with your friend, you can easily win a friend by always showing concern and respect for their opinions. You have to learn to respect their wishes, and if it clashes with yours, you all should look for a common ground to have what both of you want."

  o "If you find out that your playmate no longer wants to play your favorite game or with your favorite toy, say, *"I understand _____, but which game do you want to play?"* and wait for their response.

  o If you want to play something else or with another toy as well, tell your friend politely.

  o If both of you want to do different things, offer a truce."

- Get a child to pick a toy and stand.

- Once this is done, you go pick a toy too.

- Approach the children asking that both of you abandon their toy and play with yours. The child should insist on you all playing with them instead.

- Then begin to compromise by saying, *"All right _____, we can play with your toy for a bit, and then play with mine much later. How is that?"* Wait for the child to reply.

- If one of the children on the play mat responds in the affirmative, sit and play with them.

- Repeat with other scenarios at your disposal.

Take note of the various responses of the child at each stage and with each instruction.

Important notes:

_____

_____

_____

_____

_____

_____

_____

_____

# F. Teaching About Taking Turns

| Category of activity | Illustrative/role-playing |
|---|---|
| Objective | The idea behind this lesson is to point out to the child that partnership is the bedrock of a good friendship. Any group would love a friend who respects everyone present by allowing all persons within the group to have their turn at any game or play.<br><br>Insisting on always being the focal point or having many turns when others haven't had their turn is wrong and can hurt any friendship. It is always better to consider the needs of the other person. |
| Items to use | None |

**The Lesson**

- Begin by explaining the following to the child:

  o "When playing with another person, or a group of people, everyone desires to be given a chance to play. It is important to take your turn, and then give other people a turn also.

  o Allow other people to play while you wait.

  o Think to yourself, *"If I wait, then I will get a turn."*

  o When you wait, others will be happy with you and want to give you a turn.""

- Get a couple of children to play a game that involves taking turns.

- Instruct them to respect turn-taking in the game.

- Call the names of each participating child aloud when it's their turn to play.

- Repeat with other scenarios and games at your disposal.

Take note of the various responses of the child at each stage and with each instruction.

**Important notes:**

_____

_____

_____

_____

_____

_____

_____

_____

## G. Teaching About Playing Games

| Category of activity | Illustrative/role-playing |
|---|---|
| Objective | The idea behind this lesson is to point out to the child that playing games can be fun, but they have to be learned first.<br>Asking politely about how a game is being played and deciding who will go first can help with peer cohesion and familiarity. |
| Items to use | • A pair of dice<br>• A coin |

**The Lesson**

- Begin by explaining the following to the child:

    o "When you see your peers playing an unfamiliar game, you can always ask how to play the game.

    o Ask them by saying, "Hello, friends. *How do you play this game?*"

    o Once you have been taught how to play, decide who will go first.

    o You can be gracious by allowing the other person to go first. Say, "You can go first."

    o If there are more than two of you playing, you can play "Odd Finger Is It?" to decide who goes first.

    o You can also roll dice to decide who will go first. The person with the highest roll of the dice gets to go first.

You can also roll dice or flip a coin when it's only two of you playing.

- o  Or you can play "Odds or Evens.""

- Get a couple of children to play a game that involves taking turns.

- Instruct them to roll the dice to determine who would go first.

- You can alternatively toss a coin to determine who would play first.

> **Take note of the various responses of the child at each stage and with each instruction.**
>
> **Important notes:**
>
> _____
>
> _____
>
> _____
>
> _____
>
> _____
>
> _____
>
> _____
>
> _____

# H. Teaching About Handling Losses

| Category of activity | Illustrative/role-playing |
|---|---|
| Objective | The idea behind this lesson is to point out to the child that when playing games with friends, someone is bound to win the game. Occasionally though, the child might end up at the losing end of the game; losing doesn't feel too good and might make them upset, feel mad, or even sad. When that occurs, it's imperative to know how to deal with losing. Insisting on always winning can cause tension within the group and will always prove impossible to maintain. The best deal is to learn how to handle losing in such a way that the fun doesn't evaporate at all. |
| Items to use | None |

## The Lesson

- Begin by explaining the following to the child:

    o "When playing a game with another person or a group of people, everyone desires to win always, but this is not possible. Sometimes, you win; other times, your friends win. This doesn't mean one person is better than the others at all. It only means all the players get a chance to feel the vibes of victory and defeat."

    o "Tell yourself, *"It's only a game. There will be others."*

    o Tell yourself, *"Even if I lose the game, I can keep or win a friend if I do not get mad about losing."*

    o When you lose, tell the winner and other players, *"Good game.""*

- Get a couple of children to play a game that involves taking turns.

- Instruct them to respect turn-taking in the game.

- Call the names of each participating child aloud when it's their turn to play.

- Make the game fun by encouraging all players to give a round of applause to all, regardless of whether they win or lose.

- When you or other players lose, encourage them to say, "*Good game*" to other players.

- Repeat with other scenarios and games at your disposal.

**Take note of the various responses of the child at each stage and with each instruction.**

**Important notes:**

_____

_____

_____

_____

_____

_____

_____

_____

# I. Teaching About Forming Partnerships

| Category of activity | Illustrative/role-playing |
|---|---|
| Objective | The idea behind this lesson is to point out to the child that sometimes, what is required to get a task done is partnership. Partnering with others can breed better levels of productivity and improve on the bonds of friendship. Insisting on always doing things alone can be counterproductive. It usually is best to join forces with others to achieve much in a shorter period. |
| Items to use | A long, strong rope |

**The Lesson**

- Begin by explaining the following to the child:

    o "When playing a game with another person or a group of people, partnering with others can help in having fun and winning. When all players contribute their quota, then all are bound to have fun."

    o "Tell yourself, *"If I partner with others, the game can be more fun."*

    o When partnering, make sure to tell yourself, *"My team needs me to put in my best so that we can win.""*

- Get a couple of children to play a game.

- Divide the kids into two groups: each group holding onto one end of the rope, with a visible mark on the floor.

- Instruct them to pull until one group pulls the other in over the marking on the floor.

- Encourage each team member to put in their best, as winning would depend on partnership.

- Make the game fun by encouraging all players to give a round of applause to all, regardless of whether they win or lose.

- When you or other players lose, encourage them to say, "*Good game*" to other players.

- Repeat with other scenarios and games at your disposal.

**Take note of the various responses of the child at each stage and with each instruction.**

**Important notes:**

_____

_____

_____

_____

_____

_____

_____

_____

_____

# Chapter 5

## Social Skills Continued—Empathy and Relationship Skills

### A. Teaching About Keeping Calm

| Category of activity | Illustrative/role-playing |
|---|---|
| Objective | The idea behind this lesson is to point out to the child that sometimes, happenings ensue that give rise to feelings of anger, sadness, anxiety, or many others that are not comfortable to experience. It is important to learn how to stay calm when these circumstances come about. Inability to manage such emotions can jeopardize a friendship, partnership, or any act of fun. |
| Items to use | A long, strong rope |

**The Lesson**

- Begin by explaining the following to the child:

    o "When playing a game with another person or a group of people, you may get upset over arguments or disagreements. It is normal to feel bad when you don't have your way or when your partner yells at you, shoves you, ignores you, and so on. What is important is for you to learn how to keep calm."

- o "When you get upset, stop what you are doing and count to ten, 1…2...3...4...5...6...7...8... 9...10.

- o You can also take three deep breaths.

- o Again, you can simply begin to do something fun to make you feel better. You can draw, play a game, watch a TV show, or listen to music.

- o If none of the above helps, you can talk to someone you trust about how you feel.

  - *"I feel sad because………"*

  - *"I'm angry because………""*

- Get a couple of children to sit in a round formation on the play mat.

- Encourage them to practice counting from one to ten slowly. As they count, tell them to think about their happy moments as they do.

- Encourage the children to practice breathing exercises. As they count, tell them to think about their happy moments as they do.

- Ask the children to talk about what activities they do to calm themselves down, such as playing games, watching shows, listening to music, and so on.

- Ask the children to talk about some things that make them upset when playing with friends. Ask them how they feel after they talk about it with an adult.

**Take note of the various responses of the child at each stage and with each instruction.**

**Important notes:**

_____

_____

_____

_____

_____

_____

_____

_____

_____

## B. Teaching About Showing Understanding for the Feelings of Other People

| Category of activity | Illustrative/role-playing |
| --- | --- |
| Objective | The idea behind this lesson is to point out to the child other people do possess their state of mind that may or may not be identical to theirs. When the child learns to observe the feelings of other people and proposes to assist them, then the child is said to be "*understanding.*"<br><br>Displaying the quality of being understanding is good and helps with making and keeping friends. |
| Items to use | Two chairs |

**The Lesson**

- Begin by explaining the following to the child:

    o "When playing a game with another person or a group of people, you have to be careful to notice if your friend is feeling sad. This will help you offer help to them so that they can get back to playing and having fun."

    o "Look for indicators that other people are sad, angry, or need help.

        ▪ Look at their face.

- See if they are scowling or crying.

- Look at their body posture.

- See if they are slumping down in their chairs.

- See if they have their head down on the desks.

- See if they are wrapping their ears with their hands.

o Once you notice any of the above, ask, *"Are you all right?"* and then ask, *"What happened?"*

o Go on to ask if there is anything you can do to make them feel better. Ask, *"How can I help?"*

o If they tell you what to do, and it is within your ability, go ahead and help them.

o If what they require needs the attention of an adult, get the attention of one."

- Get a child to sit on one of the chairs.

- Instruct the child to display any emotion of sadness.

- Walk over to the child, and ask what the matter is; ask, *"Are you all right?"* and then ask, *"What happened?"*

- Ask, *"How can I help?"* Then proceed to cheer the child up.

- Once you establish that the child is OK, walk away.

- Repeat with other scenarios and games at your disposal.

> **Take note of the various responses of the child at each stage and with each instruction.**
>
> **Important notes:**
>
> _____
>
> _____
>
> _____
>
> _____
>
> _____
>
> _____
>
> _____
>
> _____

## C. Teaching About Accepting "No" for an Answer

| Category of activity | Illustrative/role-playing |
|---|---|
| Objective | The idea behind this lesson is to point out to the child that they will not always get the responses and answers that they want from other people. Sometimes, they will get a "No" for an answer.<br><br>Handling disappointments of this nature is important in building stamina toward life's challenges and toward strengthening relationships with others. We all cannot get whatever we want. |
| Items to use | None |

**The Lesson**

- Begin by explaining the following to the child:

  o "Sometimes, your friends, parents, teachers, or grown-ups may refuse to give you what you want. They might say, *"No"* when you ask them for something. This denial isn't bad in itself; this is because they might have good reasons why you shouldn't have what you requested for."

    ▪ "You may ask, *"Mom, can I have a cookie?"* and your mum might say, *"No. if you eat some, you might become too full for dinner."*

    ▪ You might ask your teacher, *"Can I go play outside in the rain?"* and your teacher might say, *"No, if you go out in the rain, you might catch a cold."*

  o When an adult tells you, *"No,"* respond with an, "OK," and do not get mad.

  o Always tell yourself, *"Adults know what's best for me. I should respect their decision."*

  o If you do not get mad, choosing to rather accept "No"for an answer, the other person will feel good about you, which may help you in getting some of what you want later."

- Get a couple of children to sit in a round formation on the play mat.

- Encourage them to talk about how they feel when they get "*No*" for an answer.

- Encourage the children to mention some good reasons that might make "*No*" good for an answer. You can begin by giving some reasons yourself.

- Ask the children to talk about what activities they can do to calm themselves down when they get mad after receiving "*No*" for an answer. *Refer to the exercise on how to keep calm.*

---

**Take note of the various responses of the child at each stage and with each instruction.**

**Important notes:**

_____

_____

_____

_____

_____

_____

_____

_____

# D. Teaching About Dealing with Mistakes

| Category of activity | Illustrative/role-playing |
|---|---|
| Objective | The idea behind this lesson is to point out to the child that everyone makes mistakes: at school, at home, when we're out at the park, restaurant, or when we travel with our parents. Some mistakes have little impact on us and others, such as adding a number wrong, while others are more dire, like ruining a sibling's toy or meddling inlies.<br><br>It's impossible to be perfect and not make mistakes; however, learning from our mistakes is the ultimate destination. |
| Items to use | None |

**The Lesson**

- Begin by explaining the following to the child:

  o "When playing with your friends on the playground, or when doing chores around the house, you make mistakes. It is normal to make mistakes every once in a while. What is important is not to make it a habit to always make mistakes and to learn from every mistake."

  o Tell yourself, *"It's OK to make a mistake. That's how we learn."*

  o If you make a mistake, try doing the task over again.

  o If you need help with the task, ask for help if you need it.

- o   Tell yourself, *"Good job learning from my mistake.""*

- Get a couple of children to sit in a round formation on the play mat.

- Ask the children to mention a few mistakes they had made in the recent past.

- Encourage them to talk about how they feel when they make mistakes.

- Encourage the children to mention how they were able to handle those mistakes when they occurred.

- Ask the children to talk about what activities they can do to calm themselves down when they get mad after making a mistake. *Refer to the exercise on how to keep calm.*

---

**Take note of the various responses of the child at each stage and with each instruction.**

**Important notes:**

_____

_____

_____

_____

_____

_____

_____

_____

---

# E. Teaching About Trying Something New

| Category of activity | Illustrative/role-playing |
|---|---|
| Objective | The idea behind this lesson is to point out to the child that every day, we get to see, hear, or do something new so that we can grow in body and mind. We can try out new clothes, foods, drinks, games, or activities.<br><br>It isn't important for us to like everything we try; some are not worth trying again. However, the important thing is that we tried them and satisfied our curiosity. |
| Items to use | <ul><li>Two chairs</li><li>A table</li><li>A board game</li></ul> |

## The Lesson

- Begin by explaining the following to the child:

    o "Everyone gets to try something new every other time, from what we eat to what types of games we play. It is important to be curious but careful about trying out new things.

    o Talk to an adult about anything you wish to try out for the first time.

    o Tell yourself, "*It's OK to try out new things. I'll learn something new once I try it.*"

    o You can begin by doing a few of your favorite activities to ease your tension.

- Watch others try it out first, so that you get an idea of how to go about it.

- You can talk to an adult about teaching you; say, *"Hi. Can you please teach me how to play this new game?"*

- Once you get a hang of the new activity, then you can try it yourself."

- Get a child to sit on one of the chairs near the table with one of their favorite board games.

- Walk over, and sit on the second chair near the table.

- Ask the child, *"Hi. Can you please show me how to play your new board game?"*

- Listen attentively, and follow your teacher, as they teach you. Follow the guidelines given above.

- Once done, say, *"Thank you for teaching me."*

- Repeat with other scenarios and games at your disposal.

Take note of the various responses of the child at each stage and with each instruction.

Important notes:

_____

_____

_____

_____

_____

_____

_____

_____

## F. Teaching About Dealing with Teasing

| Category of activity | Illustrative/role-playing |
|---|---|
| Objective | The idea behind this lesson is to point out to the child that they might come in contact with teasing from other unfriendly children. And as much as teasing is bad, it is something that the child has to learn to handle whenever it occurs.<br><br>Children need to develop mental dexterity to be able to live life to the fullest. Learning to be strong begins with handling such things as teasing and bullying. |
| Items to use | Play mat |

**The Lesson**

- Begin by explaining the following to the child:

  o "Sometimes, when playing on the playground, you might come across unfriendly kids. Some of them might tease you.

  o Teasing isn't a good thing and should never be done by anybody.

  o Once you meet a teaser, ask the person, *"Excuse me, but are you teasing*

  o Tell the person, *"I'd appreciate it if you STOP teasing me right now!"* in a strong voice."

  o If they keep on teasing, say, *"You know what? Your teasing doesn't even affect me at all."*

  o If they still keep teasing, ignore them or walk away.

  o And if the teasing continues, report to a grown-up close by."

- Get a couple of children to sit in a round formation on the play mat.

- Ask the children to mention a few times that they have individually encountered teasing.

- Encourage them to talk about their feelings when they were teased.

- Ask the children to talk about what activities they can do to calm themselves down when they get mad after being teased. *Refer to the exercise on how to keep calm.*

- Encourage the children to mention how they were able to handle those people who teased them and if what they did worked.

---

**Take note of the various responses of the child at each stage and with each instruction.**

**Important notes:**

_____

_____

_____

_____

_____

_____

_____

_____

_____

# G. Teaching About Trying When Work Is Hard

| Category of activity | Illustrative/role-playing |
|---|---|
| Objective | The idea behind this lesson is to point out to the child that life brings our way some easy-to-do things, while other things can be difficult to do, from learning subjects and topics at school to learning a new game or trying a new sport or outdoor activity.<br><br>The essential thing is to keep trying, even in the face of hardship when doing anything. This is called having perseverance. |
| Items to use | ▪ Play mat<br><br>▪ Toys that require setting up, such as a Rubik's cube or Lego toys |

## The Lesson

- Begin by explaining the following to the child:

  o "Sometimes, we all have to do something that ends up becoming hard to accomplish. Usually, anything new might look easy to handle but might turn out to be hard after all. The key is to be fearless and persevere."

  o "Begin by trying to do the work.

  o If you find that you can't do it, ask for help.

  o If you start getting upset, ask for a short time-out.

  o Once you feel rested, go back to doing your work. Try again."

- Split the children into groups of two.

- Give each group a toy or board game that has to do with assembling or arranging.

- Ask them to set up the toys by assembling or arranging them in a set amount of time.

- As they try to do the work, encourage them to ask you for help and time-outs once they feel tense.

- Encourage them to focus and persevere. If any child gives up, encourage them to help their partner complete the task. This would trigger indirect participation.

**Take note of the various responses of the child at each stage and with each instruction.**

**Important notes:**

_____

_____

_____

_____

_____

_____

_____

_____

# Chapter 6

## Social Skills Continued—Communication Games for Kids

### A. Play Telephone

| Category of activity | Games |
|---|---|
| Objective | This game is meant to sharpen the listening skills of children. By hearing and retaining what was heard before passing it on, the child is forced to focus and hear properly. |
| Items to use | Play mat |
| Number of participants | Four to ten children |

**How to play**

- Have all the children sit in a circle, with each child close enough to be able to whisper to the next child easily.

- Begin with one child; let that first child whisper a message directly into the ear of the child sitting to the right; the child would, in turn, whisper it into their neighbor's ear, and so on.

- This will continue until everyone in the circle has taken a turn.

- Once this is done, the last child to get the message can disclose it.

- More often than not, there is a high likelihood that there would be a difference between the original message and the final received message.

- You can begin with a simple message, and then gradually move to more complex sentences.

## B. Pointing Directions

| Category of activity | Games |
|---|---|
| Objective | This game helps with memory retention and focus. It involves following a drawn map to a specific location.<br><br>The children can draft out ways to reach their favorite restaurants, parks, or spaces within the school and follow those maps to locate the places. |
| Items to use | Outdoors |
| Number of participants | One |

**How to play**

- Tell the child to write down directions to their proximate favorite park or spaces within the school venue.

- Once this is done, embark on a journey along with the child, following those written directions as a map to reach there.

- As you follow the map, you can help the child understand how to improve on the written direction or add in things that, if mentioned, could help in better communication.

## C. Show and Tell

| Category of activity | Games |
|---|---|
| Objective | This game helps with memory retention and building communication. By associating words with things or topics, the child polishes their vocabulary and enriches the communication skills. |
| Items to use | Play mat |
| Number of participants | One to five |

**How to play**

- Give the child a topic, such as their favorite fruit, a favorite cartoon, or a school excursion with classmates.

- Display an item or word associated with the topic, and then ask the child to speak five lines on it.

- Once done, pick another topic. This activity can assist in furthering your kid's confidence, vocabulary, and eloquence.

## D. Picture Storytelling

| Category of activity | Games |
| --- | --- |
| Objective | This game helps the child enhance communication skills, memory retention, and problem-solving skills.<br><br>By arranging and formulating a story out of the limited pictures made available, the child is forced to think outside the box and imagine creatively. |
| Items to use | Play mat |
| Number of participants | One to five |

**How to play**

- Get a set of pictures for the child.

- Ask the child to arrange the pictures in a logical sequence.

- Ask the child to try to spin a story from it.

- On the other hand, you can get just one picture, and have the child describe the things they observe in the picture, such as the background, general public, colors, and other details.

## E. Presentation

| Category of activity | Games |
|---|---|
| Objective | This exhilarating activity will not only stimulate the oral language skills of the child but will also help them be at ease with public speaking. |
| Items to use | Play mat |
| Number of participants | One to five |

**How to play**

- Begin by proposing several themes, going from the recital of a favorite or popular poem to articulating opinions on contemporary topics such as "saving water," "recycling," "the use of gadgets," and the like.

- Ask the child to come up with a short presentation to recite to a family gathering, local park functions, or anywhere the child feels comfortable.

## F. Extempore

| Category of activity | Games |
|---|---|
| Objective | Extempore or unprompted speeches form an essential part of verbal communication and can be used to expand communication skills.<br><br>Extempore aids the child in thinking on their feet and expressing their thoughts appropriately. This activity will appropriately get the child ready for future career projections as well. |
| Items to use | Play mat |
| Number of participants | One to five |

**How to play**

- Make coupons on thought-provoking topicssuch as *"Should children's books be written by children?"*; *"Why pay attention when a person is talking"*; *"When is the best time to say, 'I'm sorry?'"*; *"What I want to be when I grow up"*; *"What to say to your friend when they are upset"*; *"How to plant a flower?"*; *"How to fix your room in 20 minutes"*; and so on.

- Have the child pick a coupon and speak on the chosen topic on the spur of the moment for a few minutes.

# G. Emotional Charades

| Category of activity | Games |
|---|---|
| Objective | This fun activity is great for assisting children in grasping diverse facial expressions, gestures, and body postures when interacting with others.<br><br>These are nonverbal communication signs that pair with verbal communication. |
| Items to use | Play mat |
| Number of participants | One to five |

**How to play**

- Give a small number of cards to the child; let each card depict a specific emotion or feeling, like anger, sadness, boredom, fatigue, or happiness.

- Have the child act them out.

- The child can likewise draw the different emotions they're likely to experience in commonplace situations.

# H. Twenty Questions

| Category of activity | Games |
|---|---|
| Objective | Twenty questions is a delightful game that supports the ability to formulate and ask direct questions in the mind of the child. <br><br> By asking intelligent questions, the child builds up communication skills as well as imagination and vocabulary. |
| Items to use | Play mat |
| Number of participants | Three to five |

**How to play**

- Instruct the children to stand in a circle.

- Allow one child to stand in the center.

- The child should think of a famous place or a known personality.

- The other children in the group can try to identify it by asking a set of twenty questions.

- The child's responses should only be *"yes"* or *"no."*

- In the event where the group cannot guess correctly, the child in the center is declared the winner.

# I. Identify the Object

| Category of activity | Games |
|---|---|
| Objective | This game of blindfolding helps with listening, focus, and vocabulary.<br><br>The children get to improve on the bonding and communication skills as they attempt to guess objects and help one another decipher what is somewhat hidden from their sight. |
| Items to use | Play mat |
| Number of participants | Four to seven |

**How to play**

- Blindfold one child, while the rest of the players select an object that can be labeled intricately for easy identification.

- Let every child take a turn in describing one feature of the chosen object.

- The blindfolded child may ask added questions as cues to help them in identifying the object.

## J. Changing the Leader

| Category of activity | Games |
|---|---|
| Objective | This game is great for training the child to understand and recognize body language indicators, which ultimately improves verbal and nonverbal communication skills. |
| Items to use | Play mat |
| Number of participants | Four to seven |

**How to play**

- Select one child as the leader; this child will do particular actions, such as stomping their feet or clapping.

- The rest of the children are to mimic the leader's actions.

- The leader then chooses another kid as the leader by smiling or winking at them.

- Other children have to identify the new leader and then replicate their actions.

Parents and caregivers who communicate regularly and proficiently with their children may be able to aid them in developing comprehensive communication skills without difficulty. Communication skills may not only offer your child improved comfort in social circumstances but can also safeguard value-added academic performances andsupport them throughout their life.

# Chapter 7

## Social Skills Continued—Problem-Solving Skills

Teaching problem-solving skills to children, especially those with either ASD or special needs can be challenging but doable. First, it all hinges on the age of the child. The methodology of coaching problem-solving skills should be adjusted as the cognitive capabilities and the size of the child's challenges expand over time.

### A. Common Approaches to Teaching Problem-Solving at Any Age

*Model effective problem-solving.*

Make it a practice to think aloud whenever you come across a challenge, as this action will be beneficial to your child. Exemplify exactly how to put to play the same problem-solving skills you desire to see your child emulate from you, especially those you are teaching them at the time. Your words and actions will give the child the real-world instances that they require, so they can apply in their own life.

Simultaneously, demonstrate to your child a preparedness to make mistakes, should they happen. Everyone comes across difficulties, and that's acceptable. From time to time, the leading solution being applied might not work at all, and that's OK too.

Once the parent makes it a habit to exemplify problem-solving skills, they become conduits for teaching the child that some things in life are out of our control. So by approaching each problem to sol ve them, we should learn to focus on the things we can control.

---

*Answer the following questions.*

*Write your child's general reactions after you started doing the following:*

1.  *When you began to think aloud:*

   _____

   _____

2.  *When you began to make mistakes in their presence:*

   _____

   _____

3.  *When you began to model the problem-solving skills you desired the child to exhibit:*

   _____

   _____

4.  *What other attitudinal changes did you observe in your child?*

   _____

5.  _____

6.  _____

7.  _____

8.  _____

---

### *Ask for advice.*

Whenever you have a challenge, endeavor to ask your kids for advice. This demonstrates to them that it's common to make mistakes and face trials. This also affords them room to practice problem-solving skills. Furthermore, by asking for their input, you show them that their ideas are valued; this will greatly assist them in gaining the confidence to try solving problems on their own.

The idea isn't to ask and not use their advice. Asking for their advice and discarding it because it doesn't make sense might have an effect that is counterproductive, as the child might feel the idea which they offered wasn't good enough. Instead, you can work with them to modify their ideas to a more practical format. Their ultimate joy would be displayed when they see their ideas at work.

*Write your child's general reactions after you started doing the following:*

1.  *How often do you ask your child for advice?*

*Often times* _____ *Not often* _____ *Not at all* _____

2.  *Why do you feel asking for their advice isn't necessary?*

_____

_____

_____

*Try asking and implementing their advice for a few days:*

3.  *Did you notice any change in the confidence of your child?*

*Yes, extremely* _____ *Not really* _____ *Not at all*

4.  *Why do you think this is now the case?*

_____

_____

_____

5.  *What other attitudinal changes did you observe in your child?*

6.  _____

7.  _____

### Don't offer all the answers.

Sometimes, one of the best ways to stir up the inner abilities of your child is for you to painstakingly allow the child to struggle and on occasion fail; this implies ultimately learning from being subjected to consequences.

This doesn't mean you're being an irresponsible parent, no not at all. You must know not to allow your child to face dire situations alone. The idea is to train the child's hands to be steady with minute challenges before allowing them to face bigger ones. It is possible to be in the shadows, guiding the child with your parental "invisible hand"; just don't be tempted to take over making the decisions and taking the steps that your child is more than ready to take.

---

*Answer the following questions.*

1. *Write your child's general reactions after you started to allow them to figure out the answers:*

_____

_____

2. *How did you deal with the child's initial fears of figuring out the answers alone?*

_____

_____

3. *What other attitudinal changes did you observe in your child?*

_____

4. _____

5. _____

6. _____

---

Now, let's focus on some strategies and activities that are age-specific. The ages itemized below are common guidelines and can be adjusted as the case might be.

## B. Three to Five Years

### Employ Emotion Coaching.

To begin with, it is important to realize that young children have to first learn to manage their emotions to step into a problem-solving mindset. In the end, it's tough for a little child to rationally reflect on solutions to a problem if they are in the middle of a tantrum. One way to go about achieving this is by employing the emotion coaching process.

Begin by teaching your kids that all sentiments are acceptable and that there are no emotions that are bad in themselves. Even apparently negative emotions such as anger, sadness, and frustration can aid in teaching valuable lessons. The most important thing is our responses to these emotions.

In addition, you can follow the processes given below:

**Name and authenticate emotions.** When your child is sad, assist them in processing the way they are feeling at the moment. Say something like, *"I understand that you're sad because Mummy had to leave early today."*

**Process each emotion.** Assist your child in finding their calming space. In the case where such a mental space doesn't exist for the child, it would be a good idea to fashion one. Allow the child to calm their body and process their emotions so they can solve problems, absorb, and grow.

**Engage them in problem-solving.** Explore possible solutions with your child, doing more listening than talking in the course of the conversation. This gives room for your child to engage and exercise their problem-solving skills; furthermore, solutions birthed from this process are more likely to be implemented by the child as they came up with those themself.

### *Ask your child to point out the hard part.*

It is very easy for children struggling on any project to quickly hit the rocks and become frustrated. At such a point, you can simply ask the child to point out to you the area that they consider to be the hard part. This helps your child in ascertaining the foundation of the challenge, making it less frightening and easier to resolve.

You can rephrase back what your child says, *"So you're saying..."* as they attempt to state the problem. Once both of you have a common grasp on the real difficulty, encourage your child to come up with solutions by saying, *"There has to be a way you can fix that..."* or *"There must be a solution you can come up with..."*

Expectedly, your child identifying the origin of the problem is likely to be able to come up with a solution. If this isn't the case, you can assist the child in exploring possible ideas and solutions. You can find innovative ways to typical *"I don't know what to* do" responses to trigger the child to think outside the box. You can ask

93

the question, *"If you DID know, what would you think?"* and see what they come up with.

### Explore problem-solving using creative play.

Free play affords sufficient occasions for navigation and creatively solving problems. This is why it is equally important to let your child pick out activities and games centered on their interests.

Characteristically, children time and again learn the most through play. Playing with items such as blocks, simple puzzles, and dress-up clothes can teach the child various processes involved in problem-solving.

The fact remains that even while engaged in play, children get involved in critical thinking. Questions such as *"Where does this puzzle piece fit?" "Where does this go?""I want to dress up as a nurse. What should I wear?" "Where did I put my action figures? Are they in the toy box?"* will help them think and come up possible solutions.

### Explore problem-solving using storybooks.

Reading age-appropriate stories that feature problems and how they are resolved by imaginary characters can help the child in formulating a healthy imagination about problem-solving and boost their confidence in approaching problems and thinking up solutions. There are a lot of books out there that can help in improving the child's problem-solving abilities; some include the following:

***Ira Sleeps Over* by Bernard Waber:** Ira is excited to sleep over at his friend Reggie's house. But there's one problem: Should he or should he not bring his teddy bear? It may look as if it's trivial, but this is the kind of primary social difficulty your child might relate to.

***Ladybug Girl and Bumblebee Boy* by Jacky Davis:** The story of two friends who want to play together but can't agree on a game to play. After taking turns coming up with suggestions, they decide on a game they both want to play.

***The Curious George Series* by Margaret and *H.A. Rey*:** A nosy little monkey gets into and out of a tight spot, teaching kids to find ways out of their own problems.

You can use such inspiring stories to connect similar events in your child's own life. You can also inquire your child about how the characters in these stories ended up solving their problems. Probe them for a variety of other solutions, discussing the possible aftermaths of each. This serves as a form of conversation reading, which aggressively engages your child in the reading experience. Intermingling with the text instead of inactively listening can turbocharge the growth of literacy skills like comprehension in preschool-aged children.

Furthermore, by asking questions about the challenges that the characters face, you can also offer significant boosts to the child's problem-solving abilities. Also, you can have your child role-play the challenge and possible solutions; this will help with reinforcing the lessons.

## C. Five to Seven Years

*Teach them problem-solving steps.*

It is advisable to formulate a simple problem-solving process for your child; make sure it is comprised of steps that are practical and worthy of consistent implementation. Here are a few steps you can explore:

- *Understanding what I am feeling:* You can assist your child in understanding what they are feeling in the moment, such as frustration, resentment, curiosity, dissatisfaction, delight, and so on. Discerning and identifying emotions can diffuse their surge, giving your child room to take a step back.

- *Understanding what the problem is:* You can help your child in identifying specific problems. On the whole, you can assist the child in taking responsibility for what comes about instead of them pointing fingers. For example, instead of saying, "Bridget got me in trouble at lunchtime," your child can say, "I got in trouble at lunchtime forquarreling with Bridget."

- *Understanding what the solutions are:* You can buoy up your child to think over as many solutions as they possibly can. As a matter of fact, the solutions do not need to be the best of the best solutions. The activity is simply a brainstorming exercise, without any forms of evaluations of the generated ideas yet.

97

- *Understanding future possibilities:* You must discuss with your child what would likely happen if they attempted to implement each of their solutions. How safe is each of the solutions? What would be its impact on the feelings of others? One way to bring this thought home is to try role-playing at this step. Your child must contemplate both the positive and negative penalties of their actions.

- *Understanding which is the best to try:* You can ask your child to choose one or more solutions to attempt. In the event that the selected solutions don't work, deliberate on why they failed before moving on to another one. Do encourage your child to keep trying until the problem is solved.

In order to have these steps embedded in memory, it is best to practice them consistently, and model solving problems of your own the same way. Always ponder on what worked, what didn't, and what can be done differently next time.

### Using craft materials in problem-solving.

One of the finest ways to indulge your child in order to boost creativity in problem-solving is by crafting. Get markers, modeling clay, cardboard boxes, tape, paper, and so on, and allow your child to go creative with them. Once occupied, children would come up with all kinds of thought-provoking creations and imaginative games with these simple materials. It is important to note that these open-ended toys aren't designed to be used in a specified right way; this allows your child to get creative and produce ideas freely.

### *Asking open-ended questions.*

When you ask open-ended questions, it advances your child's facility to contemplate analytically and creatively. This, at the end of the day, makes them better at solving problems. Instances of open-ended questions abound; some of them include:

- What was easy? What was hard?

- What do you think might happen next?

- What would you do differently next time?

- How did you figure it out? or How do you know that?

- Tell me about what you built or made.

- What do you think would happen if...?

- How can we work together to solve this?

- What did you learn from this?

One thing that makes open-ended questions exceptional is the fact that they have no right answers and can't be answered with a simple "Yes" or "No." Also, open-ended questions can be asked even when your child isn't solving any problem at the moment. This would aid the child in exercising their thinking, which will come in handy when they do have a problem to solve.

1.  What initiatives have you taken in helping your child up their problem-solving skills?

    _____

    _____

2.  Has the introduction of craft materials brought about any visible difference in the way your child now approaches problem-solving?

    _____

    _____

3.  How has using open-ended questions helped your child view challenges and how to go about solving them?

    _____

    _____

4.  What other innovative ways have you adopted that suits the growing age of your child when it comes to solving problems independently?

    _____

    _____

## D. Seven to Nine Years

*Chewing down problems into smaller masses.*

You can also help out by lending a listening ear to your child when they brainstorm, asking open-ended questions to help propel them further into creative thought when stuck.

For instance, when a child has a low grade, it is best to probe the cause by looking at the challenges in bits. Is the low grade the result of missing assignments? Or is the teacher not getting through to the child? You can ask your child to make a list of possible causes and challenge one at a time. Or, maybe tests are the concern; if so, what's bringing about the child's struggle on exams? Other reasons might be either the child is being sidetracked by friends in the class, has difficulty asking for help, or doesn't spend enough time studying at home. Once such masses or lumps are identified, you can help the child in tackling them one after the other until the problem is solved.

### *Explore simplicity, always.*

Discuss the dangers of overly embracing complications in every situation. Our society is formed in such a manner that most people, when confronted with a challenge, never pause to see the issue from the most simplistic viewpoint.

What happens when an escalator breaks down? For many people, it would mean it's time to wait for it to be fixed before they can proceed with their climb or descent. For some others, however, it is time to simply walk. Granted, there is always the temptation to think that every problem requires an out-of-the-box, pragmatic, and scientifically proven method of dealing with it, but this isn't always the case. Some problems require that we go back to the basics, to the rudimentary levels in order to find lasting solutions.

Sometimes, your child might feel stuck when facing problems; they might be tempted to stop and ask for help even before even trying to find a solution. You can buoy up your child to face challenges and work through problems instead.

---

*Answer the following questions.*

1.  *Give an instance of how you got your child to view a rather "gigantic" problem in bits and pieces and how such an approach was pivotal to resolving the problem:*

    _____

    _____

    _____

2.  *Give an instance where your child took complex approaches to problems that fundamentally had simple solutions and how you were able to guide them back to looking at the simple solutions and embracing them:*

    _____

    _____

    _____

---

## E.  Nine to Eleven Years

*Using prompts for problem-solving.*

You can get your child or a group of children items or materials such as straws, cotton balls, yarn, clothespins, tape, paper clips, sticky notes,

Popsicle sticks, etc. These kinds of prompts challenge your kids to solve problems in very  unconventional ways. You can challenge the kids to do the following:

- Make a leprechaun trap

- Fashion a jump ramp for toy cars

- Design your own game with rules

- Make a device for two people to communicate with one another

This has proven to be a fun way to exercise critical thinking and trigger creative problem-solving. In all probability, it will take quite a number of efforts to find a practical solution that works, which can apply to just about any aspect of life.

### *Using reward as a token for hard work.*

You can help your child work their way to getting stuff by having them formulate a plan to acquire the desired item themself. This activity will trigger the child to brainstorm and assess various solutions. In addition, it will help the child build more confidence.

You can also ask your child open-ended questions on how they can earn the money to acquire the item(s)they desire and buoy them up as they work toward their goal of achieving it.

### *Putting it all on paper.*

In an attempt to acquire something(s), your child can begin by putting them all down on paper, using a graphic organizer. They can then pinpoint possible problems and hindrances to acquiring such items and then think of possible solutions to overcome such hindrances.

The process can then be taken a step further: the solutions attempted can then be categorized according to those that succeeded versus those that were unsuccessful. The unsuccessful responses could further be analyzed to find out why they didn't succeed at all.

This exercise will aid the child in envisioning various outcomes and getting to know various solutions intricately, as far as workability and practicability are concerned. The lessons learned here would be beneficial when the child comes across comparable problems in the future.

---

*Answer the following questions.*

1. *How has making prompts available for your kids aided their creative and problem-solving capabilities?*

   _____

   _____

   _____

2. *Give an instance where associating reward with your child's desire to have something worked in all ramifications:*

   _____

   _____

   _____

3. *How has putting down goals on paper helped your child improve in problem-solving?*

   _____

   _____

## F. Twelve Years and Above

*Playing chess together.*

It has been statistically shown that a lot of children and teens greatly improve their problem-solving abilities when they learn and play the game of chess. Furthermore, it triggers the brain to explore the player's use of critical thinking, creativity, exploration of the board, recognition of patterns, and so on. You can start by exposing the child to books on how to play, videos, and other resources online. Of course, you the parent or guardian has to know how to play for all of this to make sense. Even though there are online versions of the game, it is recommended that both parent and child spend quality time playing the game together. This promotes cohesion between the two of you and gives the parent room to coach, monitor, and help the child in further development. If you don't know how to play, you can always learn with your teen; this will also inspire deeper connections and problem- solving together.

*Introducing them to coding.*

It is pretty normal to observe that most teens today are already tech-savvy and can put their skills to work by solving problems through learning to code. Coding stimulates creativity, logic, planning, and persistence. It isn't necessary for you as a parent to be an expert on coding before you can enroll your child, as there are a lot of great tools and online or in-person programs that can lift your child's coding skills.

*Inspiring them to take on an evocative project.*

You can encourage your teen to take up a project that they cherish personally. This project must hold great meaning to them, such as starting a YouTube channel. As they try to navigate around the various challenges that might accompany venturing into such projects, your teen will practice problem-solving skills in many different ways and at very consistent levels, which all breeds better performances in the child.

*Exploring the SODAS method.*

SODAS is an acronym for a number of steps necessary to take when attempting to solve a problem. These steps can be employed when tackling either big or small problems. This simple acronym is:

- **S**ituation

- **O**ptions

- **D**isadvantages

- **A**dvantages

- **S**olution

There are a number of games and activities that you can draft your teen into that require them to follow this method in order to solve problems that arise.

*Buoying them up to connect with problem-solving groups.*
Encouraging your teen to become a part of problem-solving groups

is important in many ways. First, it will help them grow and sustain a healthy appetite for problem-solving. Second, they will meet with other teens and share brilliant ideas. Third, they get to grow their collection of "great ideas" in a very short time. Fourth, they never get to face their seemingly insurmountable problems alone. Their fellows within the group can help inspire them and lend helping hands where necessary. So, does your teen relish solving problems in a team? Then get them to join a group or club that helps them improve their skills in a multiplicity of sceneries, from science and robotics to debating and international affairs. Below are a few instances of groups that your child can explore and choose from; this list is in no way exhaustive:

- Odyssey of the Mind

- Model U.N.

- Debate team

- Science Olympiad

Granted, some of the recommendations above might be too far-reaching when it comes to grooming children with ASD or special needs. However, these recommendations are practical and can be applied in varying proportions, depending on the level of growth of the child.

The idea is to groom the children, regardless of the level of mental or physical affliction, to enable them to lead healthy lives even when the parent or guardian isn't around. By applying these recommendations, you give the child the opportunity required to improve and tap into their hidden talents. One action can trigger phenomenal growth and improvements in another area. Parents simply have to keep the faith and keep the train moving.

---

**Answer the following questions.**

1. *How has playing chess with your ward improved their ability to think critically?*

   _____

   _____

2. *Have you noticed any forms of improvements in your child's problem-solving abilities since you exposed them to coding?*

   _____

   _____

3. *What has been the level of maturity of your child since they took up a passionate project?*

   _____

   _____

4. *Give an instance where you inspired your child to apply SODAS*

   _____

   _____

5. *What problem-solving group(s) has your child joined recently, and how has it improved their passion for problem-solving?*

   _____

   _____

---

# Chapter 8

## Social Skills Continued—Accountability

Teaching kids personal accountability implies teaching them to right their wrongs, whether or not someone is watching. It has to do with teaching children about the imminent possibility of making mistakes in life, but in the event where such mistakes happen, then they are expected to rise and make amends the best way they can. Children have a knack for thinking that only their parents can and should take responsibility for their actions. While this might be the case when it has to do with the children's general upkeep and protection (which in the real sense, is *the* parents taking responsibility for *their* actions), children need to be taught to understand personal responsibility and accountability as they will not remain children forever.

Unlike many traits, responsibility isn't inborn, and it also isn't much fun to learn either. Most responsibilities take up a lot of time and are boring for a child. Kids, on the other hand, seek exhilaration and do their best to stay away from boring things such as cleaning their room, making their bed, putting their books away, or doing their homework.

But it must be understood that it takes a lot of self-control and development for a kid to stay on a task, especially when such a task isn't fun. It takes a lot of practice and necessitates ample parental coaching for the child to be responsible. You have to hold your child accountable for their responsibilities.

Below are a few ways to go about developing accountability in your child. This will help guide them to be functional and independent adults in the future.

## A. Make a Habit of Enforcing Accountability

Assumedly, most parents do try to trigger a sense of responsibility within their growing kids. They tell them to do the dishes, clean up their rooms, do their chores, and so on. However, the challenge isn't in the reeling out of instructions by parents to their wards but in their reactions when they learn that their instructions have been flouted by the child. In other words, even though they give instructions, parents don't always promote accountability, and that's where the error is. Accountability has to be enforced by parents, guardians, caregivers, and teachers.

It is extremely necessary to hold your kids accountable for not meeting their responsibilities. Being held accountable necessitates that the parent makes the consequence not as good as when the child does complete the task in the first place. This act of being held accountable espouses a disposition to meet the responsibilities next time.

Regrettably, a lot of parents either don't hold their kids accountable or don't finish off on the consequences once they set them, which in turn simply encourages more irresponsibility. Again, the child learns that staging excuses, lies, and justifications can serve as escape points for them in their effort to avoid responsibility for themself or their behavior.

Furthermore, the child learns that possessions do not have to be earned and that society, as characterized by their parents, won't follow through and hold them accountable. This in itself is a terrible lesson to learn. So it becomes crucial to teach kids how to be responsible, and if they flaunt directives and instructions, you have to hold them accountable.

---

*Answer the following questions.*

1. *How often have you followed through with consequences set for your child if they fail to meet with responsibility?*

*Always_____ Not always_____ rarely_____Never_____*

2. *How have your actions or inactions as far as doling out the consequences for failing to meet responsibility affected the attitude and development of your child when it comes to accountability?*

    _____

    _____

3. *Write a list of consequences that you feel might trigger your child toward being responsible.*

    _____

    _____

4. *Give an instance where your following through with consequence yielded the right results.*

    _____

    _____

---

## B. Start Teaching Accountability Early

It is important for your child to begin to learn about accountability at an early age. As a parent, have them begin taking responsibility for whatever endeavor they're involved with. For example, have your child put their toys away before dinner. Now, if the child finds it hard focusing on the task due to them being too young, you can help by getting down on the floor and picking up some of the toys along with the child. But don't do it all for them; you can say, "I'll do one, and then you do one." This will teach the child to take care of their responsibilities.

Another thing you can introduce early into your child's life is an alarm clock. An alarm helps them learn the duty of setting the alarm at night and then getting up and shutting it off. This points out to them in clear terms that they're an individual and that they have responsibilities.

1.  How early in your child's life did you introduce accountability?

Very early (0–2)_____    early enough (3–6)_____    not quite early
(7–12)_____ quite late (12 and above)_____

2.  How has introducing them to accountability at the time you did
    played out in their general outlook to responsibility?

    _____

    _____

3.  Write a list of occasions where you insisted the child be accountable
    no matter what.

    _____

    _____

4.  Give an instance where your following through with your choice
    yielded the right results.

    _____

    _____

## C. Make a Habit of Naming Responsibilities Using Responsible Language

You can find a way of always pinpointing responsibility when it is
done or when issuing out instructions, mentioning it in clear
sentences and conversations.

For instance, once your child completes a task, say, *"Nice job
following through on your responsibility." "I appreciate the way
you handled that responsibility." "You know, it's your responsibility
to do that, and I'm happy that you did it." "You know, I'm
rewarding you because you met your responsibility."*

In other words, the more you pinpoint it, the more mindful your child becomes of it. It is also important that the child realizes that they are being rewarded for completing their responsibility, not for being cute, adorable, or friendly. The earlier you verbalize and connect rewards to responsibilities, the more clearly that becomes associated in the mind of your child.

---

*Answer the following questions.*

1. *Come up with a list of sentences that identifies and highlights the word "responsibility" that you can use while talking to your child about accountability.*

   _____

   _____

   _____

   _____

   _____

2. *How have you been able to help your child closely associate responsibility to reward?*

   _____

   _____

   _____

   _____

   _____

3. *Give an instance where such a kind of association yielded the right results.*

   _____

   _____

   _____

   _____

## D. Make a Habit of Setting the Example

It is expected that parent should meet their responsibilities every so often and not hesitate to label them when they do. This means you can say, *"My responsibility is to go to provide for the family, and I'm doing it today."* Another instance could be you responding to the question from your child about where you are going with: *"I'm going to work. That's my responsibility."* *"I'm going grocery shopping. That's my responsibility."*

Your modeling good behavior can help reinforce accountability skills in your child. You have to strive to be an example. As a parent, when you make a promise to your child that you are going to do something, that thing becomes your responsibility to do. This implies that it would be more ideal for you to only make promises that you intend and can keep. Also, remember that when you meet responsibilities, you should make sure to use language that says so.

*Answer the following questions.*

1. *How often do you model responsibility to your child?*

*Very often_____ often enough_____ not quite often_____ not at all_____*

2. *How has the idea of modeling accountability affected the perceptions of your child in the general outlook to responsibility?*

_____
_____
_____
_____

3. *Write a list of occasions where you modeled accountability.*

_____
_____
_____
_____

4. *Give an instance where your example inspired your child toward being responsible.*

_____
_____
_____
_____

## E.  Take the Time to Teach and Coach Responsibility

It is important for you as a parent to find time to sit down and explain to your child(ren) what responsibility means. Responsibilities are similar to commitments or promises; they are the things that a person must do, the things that are on one's shoulder to manage, and the things you're saddled with, where other people are looking up to you to accomplish.

Parents need to tell their wards that once responsibility is left undone, the act lets down a lot of people and presents a bad image of the child to others. So it is important to take responsibility, no matter what. Make it clear that, *"If you play with your toys, it's your responsibility to put them away."* Or for an older child, say, *"If you make a sandwich for yourself, it's your responsibility to clean up after yourself."*

Train your child into meeting their responsibilities. It is very important for you to coach your kids and not just lecture them to. A coach typically doesn't go out onto the pitch and does the playing for players. Instead, coaches work with the players from the sidelines, instructing and inspiring instead of criticizing.

In the same way, you must coach your kids about their responsibilities. Criticism has its place in life, but with kids, it can be counterproductive as it only makes them defensive when you start to scold them about something that didn't get done right.

117

1. How often do you sit with your child to talk about accountability and responsibility?

*Very often_____     often enough_____     not quite often_____*
*not at all_____*

2. Write a list of occasions where you coached your child on accountability.

_____

_____

_____

_____

3. Give an instance where your coaching helped inspire your child toward being responsible.

_____

_____

_____

_____

## F. Employ the Use of Rewards and Consequences

It is always advised to associate responsibility with both rewards and consequences. You can say to the child, *"You're getting this reward because you cleaned up the car." "This is your reward for doing your schoolwork." "This is your reward for keeping your room neat all day."*

In the same vein, say to your child, *"This is the consequence for not doing your chores this morning." "This is the consequence for not finishing your homework.*" "You're *getting this consequence because you didn't clean your room.*"

On some occasions, parents can have a sit-down with their kids and draft up a list of rewards and consequences. How can you hold kids accountable? You can use items and actions that can serve as effective consequences. You can hold back things like electronics or allocate additional chores or extra work. In addition, you can give them task-oriented consequences.

As for rewards, you can draw up a rewards menu. Rewards should not be limited to handing down cash or buying things. You can explore other activities that are fun and healthy, such as taking walks, going to the park, or maybe visiting the beach. You could reward them with playing catch or spending time with the child at the swing.

You can say to your child, "*You know, you did well today. I'm going to take you down to the beach this Saturday.*"

Rewards don't have to be expensive; they are simply tokens of gratitude. So use your imagination. For older children, you can go by the river, go hiking, go to the park, go downtown, or give more screen time. For teens, you can reward them with later bedtimes or more time with their friends. Adolescents can be rewarded with getting away from you and being on your own, and that's OK.

1. *How often do you use rewards and consequences as tokens of being accountable and responsible?*

*Very often_____often enough_____ not quite often_____ not at all_____*

2. *Write a list of rewards you can use to help your child work hard at being responsible.*

_____

_____

_____

_____

3. *Write a list of consequences you can use to spur your child at being responsible.*

_____

_____

_____

_____

## G. Make Sure You and Your Kid are on the Same Page

Once you decide to change your approach in teaching responsibility and accountability, it is important that you talk with your kids, so that you all are on the same page as touching what changes to expect and new paths to tread from then on. Find a suitable time, and say to your kids individually,

*"From now on, I'm going to start to point out how we meet responsibilities around here. That way, you'll have a clearer knowledge of how many responsibilities I meet and why I think you must meet your responsibilities too."*

120

*"All the things that I buy for you as a parent, you're going to have to get for yourself in the future. And to do that, you're going to have to be able to meet responsibilities just like I do. And if I didn't meet my responsibilities of going to work and doing a good job, I would not be able to give you those things."*

Endeavor to employ simple, straight talk that moves from "this is why responsibilities are important" to "here's what's going to happen if you do—or if you don't—meet your responsibilities."

---

*Answer the following questions.*

*Formulate a "here is what is going to happen here on in" speech outlining why responsibility is important and what's going to happen if you do—or if you don't—meet your responsibilities.*

_____

_____

_____

_____

_____

_____

_____

_____

_____

Learning how to meet responsibilities and be accountable is one of the most vital skills children ought to learn while they are still young. As they grow older, they'll have an in-depth grasp of the connection between responsibilities, accountability, and rewards. But it's never too early or too late to learn. It is imperative for children who didn't learn to meet responsibilities at an early age to learn them at whatever age their parents get ready to teach them.

In the event that children cultivate personal responsibility, they get their best chance of circumventing a lot of the pitfalls of life. It makes them more equipped to deal with unavoidable difficulties that arise in life, for the most part, as they get older.

It is ideal to simply *expect* your child to act responsibly, but it is recommended that you *require* such behavior, even *demand, teach,* and *coach* it. However, it is required of parents to be considerate about how to go about enforcing accountability; enforcement should never spill into abuse. You should have in mind that accountability is a part of growing up, and is an essential component of learning how to function in an ever more complex and challenging world.

# Chapter 9

## Friendship Skills

Friendship and social play skills are important proficiencies for young kids to cultivate in the early years of school, as they form the groundwork for long-standing success in school and the community. As parents and teachers who handle children every day, it is important for us to help them learn how to connect with others and make lasting friendships. Social skills can be argued by some to be more important than academic or athletic skills, and thus should be given optimum value. At schools, however, very little or no time is dedicated to teaching these vital skills, but for children who have challenges with social skills deficits, this attention is indeed vital.

Deficits in social skills are associated with a lot of problems for children, youths, and adults, while healthy social skills are linked with a myriad of positive life outcomes. Therefore, it is incumbent upon parents and teachers to teach social skills to their wards. In an inclusive classroom, teachers may probably have students who need some added care in developing and strengthening these skills.

But the question still stands: where do we start? As far as learning how to make friends is concerned, there are many outlets to achieving this feat. It ranges from social activities to play and games. Below are a few ways to encourage friendship skills and social play. These ideas were developed to build social and communication skills for students with autism, but they'll also have benefits for a wide range of learners. Give these a try in your classroom, and see which ones are most helpful to your students.

## A. Exploring Essential Friendship Skills for Children

We will explore a few friendship skills that every child requires in order to build long-lasting relationships and friendships. These skills can and must be taught if the child is to experience relative ease in bonding with their peers in school and later in life.

### *Locate the right kinfolk.*

One of the most essential friendship skills is the aptitude to determine who might be a good friend. Children need to find other kids who agree to take them for who they are, who think of them as equals, and who share some of the same interests. Some children attempt to join the groups that they perceived to be "popular" only to discover that they are not truly at home, as such friendships are disproportionate and unrewarding. Time and again, only one child, typically the one not being accepted, thinks of the friendship as viable, and therefore is devoted to it. Instead of urging children to go on forcing themselves into a friendship or group where they are not unreservedly wanted, you can help them to find out where their real kinfolk are, which may be just one or two other compatible kids.

### Wear a brilliant smile.

It is a fact that nonverbal communications are potent. This is why you should teach your children to wear a brilliant smile, stand up straight, give eye contact, give a firm handshake, and have an open stance when talking to others. These will all add to why other people would naturally perceive them as friendly and welcoming. Children who think others are being mean or outrightly ignoring them every so often are not conscious of how they are perceived by those people. So, children need to learn that by keeping a warm smile and giving away a positive appearance, more people will be paying attention to them as a potential friend.

### Ask the right questions.

It is common for children to be too carried away talking about themselves. However, asking good questions frequently serves as the access point for structuring lasting friendships. You can help your child think about what types of questions they might ask. Questions can range from sports, video games, academic, music, art, and television shows to fun activities.

*"Do you play any instruments?""What do you like to do after school?""What's your favorite TV game show?" "What are you having for lunch?""How many brothers and sisters do you have?" "Who's your science teacher?"*

Furthermore, you can practice at the dinner table by role-playing as a potential friend, and have your child ask some questions. Naturally, going along with asking questions is attending to the answer and asking follow-up questions. Children who get the hang of asking questions, listening, and following up are trendy. This is because they give others the occasion to share about themselves.

### Learn to invite; learn to join.

Naturally, the origin of the beginning of any friendship is the bold attempt by someone to take action. This can be one person inviting another to do something fun or it can be joining in with what a child or group is already doing. Begin by clarifying this idea to your child before going on to think about simple, low-risk invitations:

*"Do you want to play basketball or something else after school?"* *"Can I sit next to you?""Do you want to play with my action figures?"* *"Would you like to come over after school?"*

A different way to bond is for the child to ask to join a game. It's essential for the child to be aware of the fact that it's not always suitable to ask to join, as it might not be well received if it interrupts the flow of play. On occasion, in the middle of a game, it's tough to try to draft in a new player. So, instead of asking to join right then, the child can evaluate what others are doing and say, *"Hey, can I play the next game?"* rather than interrupting at the halfway point.

### Learn to share.

Sharing is an essential social skill that improves friendships when done accordingly. However, once done poorly or not done at all, it can function as a social repellant. Children do need help when it comes to learning how to share their toys, books, markers, and so on.

Furthermore, as children get older, they have to be taught how to share information about themselves in a fashion that doesn't present them as being boastful but helps others in getting to know them. It is acceptable for the child to share about themselves, so that the other person would get to know them, but they also have to ask questions and listen to what others have to say. They must learn to share the spotlight; it is a critically important skill. They should learn to allow others to be in the high beam sometimes.

### Be happy for the victories of friends.

One friendship-enhancing skill that every child must learn is how to respond positively to the triumphs of others. Research has established that this act also improves matrimonies and other forms of relationship. Your child has to master the art of being truly happy and excited for the victories and achievements of their friends, and this must flow as though they shared in such a victory. It doesn't matter if their friends beat them in a race or get a better grade on a test. What they should never allow to arise is the feeling of jealousy. Instead, they should learn to celebrate and congratulate their friend; this would be great for the friendship. When we truthfully celebrate the accomplishments of others, our connections with them get stronger; with a bit of luck, the friend gives in return by being happy for us and our victories.

### Cultivate coping approaches for difficult emotions.

Empirical research centered on which children are most liked by peers and which children are unpopular or overruled, self-regulation-difficulty in handling emotions seems to be the biggest repellant. Children who lash out or react excessively to negative situations just aren't enjoyable to be around and are often disliked by peers. Therefore, children who find it hard to regulate and act on their feelings must learn to manage tough emotions productively.

### Try resolving conflicts, and solve problems by yourselves.

Children who make it a habit to run to an adult every time they get their feelings hurt or who can't solve a problem with a peer need to be taught how to resolve their conflicts. They unambiguously need to learn how to react to bantering, hostile comments, losing, finger-pointing, being left out, and peer pressure. Going over different ways to manage conflicts and solve problems can help children learn vital life and relationship skills.

### Learn how to empathize.

Empathy is a social skill that is not that easy to either define or teach. In general, empathy is our ability to perceive the emotions of other people and imagine what they may be thinking or feeling. Empathic responses are standard-issue, grown-up social skills; nevertheless, even adults have trouble with them. If adults struggle with empathy, how much more problematic must it be for children!

But then again self-awareness, self-regulation, and the ability to take another's standpoint are all skills children must come to recognize.

### Train on kindness.

Some children are unsurprisingly kind and giving to others, but most need help cultivating their kindness skills. There are a lot of ways to teach kindness; giving to others can be an ideal start. Remarking favorably on others is also a great way to express kindness and a good skill to exercise.

## Answer the following questions:

1. From the above chapter, what can you identify as the virtues lacking in your child/ward?

_____

_____

_____

2. What are some of the approaches you adopted in the quest to encourage your child to develop better friendship skills?

_____

_____

_____

3. Discuss with your child, and pinpoint areas where they still struggle to master from the above chapter.

_____

_____

_____

# Chapter 10

## Friendship Skills Continued—Activities and Games that Enhance Friendship Skills

### A. The Greeting Game

| Category of activity | Game |
| --- | --- |
| Objective | This game will help in loosening up the children as they get to know each other. This game will expose the kids in a manner in which they will quickly overcome their shyness. They will also subconsciously imbibe the virtue of greeting other people whenever they meet them. |
| Items to use | A play mat |

**How to play**

- Have every child sit down on the play mat on the floor forming a circle.

- Have everyone in the group take a turn going around the circle and saying, "Hello." Make sure they do so with a brilliant smile on their faces.

- Have everyone cheer for the child who successfully greets everyone.

- Allow any children with ADS or children with special needs to watch one or two other children take a turn before giving them a chance to go around the circle greeting peers.

## B. The Tag Game

| Category of activity | Game |
|---|---|
| Objective | This game will help with partnership and collaboration development. The child will learn to see their peers as helping agents that they ought to befriend. It will also help with overcoming shyness. |
| Items to use | None |

**How to play**

- Begin by arranging the kids to form a straight line.

- The first child on the line should tag the kid behind them and let the tagging continue until the last child is tagged.

- The last child on the line should then run to the front of the line

- The last kid who is now the first should tag the kid behind them and let the tagging continue till it gets to the last kid on the line.

- This tagging should continue until every kid has made it to the front and back of the line at one time or another.

- For learners who have ADS or children with special needs to join, have them watch the group play for a while, and then encourage them to join the game.

- You can prompt them to ask, "Can I play?" and then prompt them to join in.

- Fade away your prompts, as the child becomes more independent in joining in the game.

Take note of the various responses of the child at each stage and with each instruction.

Important notes:

_____

_____

_____

_____

_____

_____

_____

_____

## C. The Group Mural

| Category of activity | Game |
| --- | --- |
| Objective | This game will help with partnership and collaboration development. The child will learn to see their peers as partners and would greatly benefit from their inputs. It will also help in loosening up the child around other people. |
| Items to use | <ul><li>Mural paper</li><li>Art materials, such as paint, paint brushes, markers, glitter, stickers, and stencils</li></ul> |

**How to play**

- Tape a large piece of mural paper to a table.

- Ask for suggestions for a theme, such as St. Patrick's Day, Spring, All about Me, or The Farm.

- Set out art materials.

- Limit the number of each type of supply; this will make the group practice sharing and turn-taking.

- For kids who don't like to get their hands muddled, have bowls of warm water or wet paper towels readily available and give a smock to every person.

- Ask the group to work together to complete the mural.

- Once the activity is over, have them work together on the cleanup.

Take note of the various responses of the child at each stage and with each instruction.

Important notes:

_____

_____

_____

_____

_____

_____

_____

_____

## D. Puzzle Together

| Category of activity | Game |
|---|---|
| Objective | This game will help the child partner with others. It triggers intellectual and language skills as well. Furthermore, it helps with development of collaboration and friendship skills. |
| Items to use | <ul><li>Table and two chairs</li><li>Puzzle board and pieces</li></ul> |

# How to play

- Place a chair on either side of a table.

- Put two empty puzzle boards on one chair and the puzzle pieces on the other.

- Ask your child to pick a peer partner, and then make them sit down at the table.

- The child sitting in front of the puzzle pieces can give them to the partner, one at a time until they both complete the puzzle.

- You can then switch roles for the kids; let the one who arranged the puzzle be told to pass the pieces to their partner this time around.

---

**Take note of the various responses of the child at each stage and with each instruction.**

**Important notes:**

_____

_____

_____

_____

_____

_____

_____

_____

# E.  Class Detectives

| Category of activity | Game |
| --- | --- |
| Objective | This game will help the child partner with others. It triggers intellectual and language skills as well. Furthermore, it helps with the development of collaboration and friendship skills. |
| Items to use | Class attendance log |

**How to play**

- Hide an item someplace in the classroom (such as the attendance log).

- Invite your students to play detective together to find the hidden item.

- Encourage them to talk to each other and share ideas.

- You can spice things up by placing clues here and there. The complexity of the clues can vary depending on the ages of your students.

Take note of the various responses of the child at each stage and with each instruction.

Important notes:

_____

_____

_____

_____

_____

_____

_____

_____

_____

## F. Building Together

| Category of activity | Game |
|---|---|
| Objective | This game is a fun way for kids to work together as partners and as friends. It helps with bonding and triggers intellectual and language skills as well. |
| Items to use | Lego toys |

**How to play**

- Tell the children to build something together with Legos or blocks.

- For learners who are children with special needs, you can ask them to place the first block, and then have the peer place the next block.

- Set up a turn-taking routine between the two of them.

- When their masterpiece is completed, have them work together to return the blocks to the marked bin.

| Take note of the various responses of the child at each stage and with each instruction. |
|---|
| Important notes: |
| _____ |
| _____ |
| _____ |
| _____ |
| _____ |
| _____ |
| _____ |
| _____ |

# G. Help Reach Out for Play

| Category of activity | Play |
|---|---|
| Objective | Some of your students may need assistance with inviting peers to play a game or activity with them. This activity will enable them to get help in joining other playmates during playtime. This form of assistance will help them realize the place of partnership and friendship. |
| Items to use | Lego toys |

## How to play

- Have your student watch the others play, and then ask the learner, "Where would you like to play?"

- For learners who are children with special needs, you can ask them to place the first block, and then have the peer place the next block.

- Set up a turn-taking routine between the two of them.

- When their masterpiece is completed, have them work together to return the blocks to the marked bin.

- Encourage your student to go to the preferred activity area and ask a peer to play. The child can use words, a picture card, or a sign.

- Keep on encouraging the student to let other peers join in the fun, either by verbally saying, "Yes," affirming with the shaking of the head, signaling for the peer to join, or giving a picture card to the peer.

- Fade the urgings, as the child becomes more successful.

> **Take note of the various responses of the child at each stage and with each instruction.**
>
> **Important notes:**
>
> _____
>
> _____
>
> _____
>
> _____
>
> _____
>
> _____
>
> _____
>
> _____
>
> _____

## H. Playing Video Games

| Category of activity | Play |
|---|---|
| Objective | Video or computer games are fun ways for children to learn. You can use these to teach various virtues and skills. The child would learn partnership, patience, awareness, and friendship. |
| Items to use | A video or computer game |

**How to play**

- Set up your game station with two chairs.

- Use a *"wait"* picture to show who is waiting to play the computer game next.

- If you are using a laptop computer, set up one mouse and two mouse pads. Put the mouse on the pad of the child going first and a *"wait"* picture on the pad of the other person.

- Place a visual timer improved with audio where both students can see it. Set the timer for five minutes as the first person begins to play.

- Encourage your student to go to the preferred activity area and ask a peer to play. The child can use words, a picture card, or a sign.

- Keep on encouraging the student to let other peers join in the fun, either by verbally saying, "Yes," affirming with the shaking of the head, signaling for the peer to join, or giving a picture card to the peer.

- If you notice that the other child is having a hard time waiting, simply remind them, *"It's Peter's turn; you have to wait."*

- Refer the child to the picture, or point to the moving timer.

- When the bell rings, say, *"Peter's turn is all done. Now it's your turn, Bob."*

- Have the children exchange pictographs, and reset the timer for five minutes.

Take note of the various responses of the child at each stage and with each instruction.

Important notes:

_____

_____

_____

_____

_____

_____

_____

_____

_____

## I. Getting Dramatic

| Category of activity | Play |
|---|---|
| Objective | Dramatic play can be a great way to build social skills and spark friendships.<br>For children who are interested in music, you can use their interest to help build social play skills. |
| Items to use | None |

**How to play**

- Have your students recreate a story with a group using action figures.

- They can also dress up as favorite characters and act out a familiar story with a group.

- They can also participate in a puppet show or act out a role with peers using a scenario they both understand and agree upon.

*For children who are interested in music, the following can be done:*

- Have them play musical chairs with a group.

- Alternatively, you can have them participate in a musical *Hot Potato* game with a beanbag.

- Again, you can have them take turns following the musical pattern of the game Simon.

- You can also have them play an instrument as part of a marching band or listen to audio tracks with peers.

**Take note of the various responses of the child at each stage and with each instruction.**

**Important notes:**

_____

_____

_____

_____

_____

_____

_____

_____

_____

When putting up social play activities in your classroom, it is quite useful to gradually build up the convolution and difficulty of each play. You can begin with analogous activities in which the children with special needs have their own set of materials, and then bring in structured, predictable activities with a clear set of rules. Then, as the child learns to take part in these activities, you can move on to support more cooperative play with peers.

# Chapter 11

## Life Skills

The world today is giving children so many things to explore and learn from; with all these, it is increasingly possible for them to miss out on hands-on life skills, from running a load of wash, reading a map, to drafting a handwritten letter.

A new study indicated that while 78 percent of children ranging from ages three to five living in the United States can circumnavigate a smartphone, only about 15 percent could make their breakfast. This is partly because many parents would rather do everything for their children instead of allowing them to figure out how to take care of themselves. It is extremely vital to start coaching our children on these life skills right away and put the kid on the path toward independence.

The question remains: are you as a parent getting your child ready to be independent?

Teaching your child life skills is not only essential for self-care and competence but also so that the child can feel enabled, work on socialization and reasoning, and grow to develop a healthy self-esteem.

Below is a table of age-appropriate skills aimed at helping get your child ready for each stage of their life, from preschool until the day they fly the pen.

| Ages | The expected level of life skill | Ability |
|---|---|---|
| Ages two to three | Minor chores and rudimentary cleaning *(This is the age when your child will begin to learn simple life skills)* | By the age of three, your child should be able to<br><br>• assist in putting their toys away.<br>• dress (with enough assistance from you).<br>• put their clothes in the basket when they undress.<br>• clear their plate after meals.<br>• help in setting the table.<br>• brush their teeth and wash their face with plenty of help. |
| Ages four to five | Key names and numbers *(Safety skills are high on the list now)* | By the age of five, your child should be able to<br><br>• know their full name, address, and phone number to reach you.<br>• know how to place an emergency call.<br>• know how to carry out simple cleaning chores such as cleaning easy-to-reach areas and clearing the table after meals.<br>• feed pets.<br>• ascertain money denominations and understand the very basic idea of how money is used.<br>• brush their teeth, comb their hair, and wash their face without assistance.<br>• help with basic laundry chores, |

| | | |
|---|---|---|
| | | like putting their clothes away and bringing their dirty clothes to the laundry. <br> • choose their clothes to wear. |
| **Ages six to seven** | Basic cooking techniques <br> *(Kids at this age can start to help with cooking meals)* | By the age of seven, your child should be able to <br> • mix, stir, and cut with a dull knife. <br> • make a basic meal, such as a sandwich. <br> • help put the groceries away. <br> • wash the dishes. <br> • use basic household cleaners safely. <br> • clean up the bathroom after using it. <br> • make their bed without assistance. <br> • bathe unsupervised. |
| **Ages eight to nine** | Pride in personal belongings <br> *(By this time, your child should take pride in their possessions and take care of them appropriately)* | By the age of nine, your child should be able to <br> • fold their clothes. <br> • learn simple sewing. <br> • care for outdoor toys such as their bike. <br> • take care of personal hygiene without being told to do so. <br> • use a broom and dustpan properly. <br> • read a recipe and prepare a simple meal. <br> • help create a grocery list. <br> • count and make change. <br> • take out the trash. |

147

| | | |
|---|---|---|
| **Ages ten to thirteen** | Gaining independence *(Ten is about the age when your child can begin to perform many skills independently)* | By the age of thirteen, your child should be able to<br><br>• stay home alone.<br>• go to the store and make purchases by themself.<br>• change their bedsheets.<br>• use the washing machine and dryer.<br>• plan and prepare a meal with several ingredients.<br>• use the oven to broil or bake foods.<br>• read labels.<br>• iron clothes.<br>• use basic hand tools.<br>• look after younger siblings or neighbors. |
| **Young Adults** | Preparing to live on their own<br>*(Your child will need to know how to support themself when they go away to college or move out)* | There are still a few skills they should know before venturing out on their own, including the following:<br><br>• make regular doctor and dentist appointments and other important health-related appointments<br>• have a basic understanding of finances, and be able to manage their bank account, pay a bill, and use a credit card<br>• understand basic contracts, like an apartment or car lease<br>• schedule oil changes and basic car maintenance |

**It is expected that before your child heads to college, they should have mastered these six life skills to convincing levels.**

# Chapter 12

## Life Skills Continued

One question worth asking is:how independent is your child? This is a question worth asking yourself. We need to prove ourselves as a parent on whether or not our children can look after themselves if left alone for a while, or if they are sufficiently equipped with critical life skills to face the world.

It is without question important for children to learn more than just academically, and getting them enrolled in various activity classes might not be enough either. Life skills education solely cannot stop with the level of contact your child gets in school. They need to be taught at home through experiences and training activities.

If you desire for your child to grow up strong, you have to teach by example. Being a parent isn't easyat all. More so, it's even more problematic working on self-improvement while raising a child. So let's first look at a few skills that are critical for any growing child to learn for them to find it easy to deal with adulthood when it comes.

## A. Basic Life Skills to Equip Your Child With

*Teach them basic self-defense.*

In today's world, safety is of paramount importance, and learning basic self-defense makes the child feel more independent as well as more confident. Learning basic self-defense is essential, whether it's for your son or your daughter. These days, a lot of schools participate in teaching basic self-defense to children. You can always get external help for your kids if their schools don't offer such kinds of skill training.

The idea of this skill development isn't to turn your child into a lethal fighter, but to teach them basic defense routines that they can apply when they are in danger, from running to a safe zone, blowing a rape whistle, and escaping from a chokehold to restraining an enemy.

*Teach them first aid and the importance of health*

It is impossible to always be around whenever your child gets hurt, bitten, or develops a rash. So it is wise to empower them such that they can take care of themselves and others in case of an emergency until a grown-up arrives.

This is, for all intents and purposes, something that all schools should cover, but most do not. So, it is strongly recommended that it be reinforced at home. This you can do by teaching your child essential first-aid steps, showing them a first-aid kit and its contents.

Another essential skill is teaching your child to take care of their health. Do not just insist that they eat vegetables; instead, take time out to discuss with them the health risks of eating junk food all the time. In addition, explain to them how the healthy food will benefit them in a way that they can apply to themselves. For instance, if your child is interested in sports, talk about foods that promote increased stamina and agility, enabling them to play better at their sport.

For children that care about physical looks such as, teeth and hair, tell them about the importance of brushing regularly, omega-3 fatty acids, and the foods that contain them.

### *Teach them to do their work.*

There is a danger hovering over a child that isn't taught responsibility and daily living skills today; this is because it would become a problem for them in the future when they grow up and leave home to pursue their education or career.

Regrettably, most parents today are consumed with running around doing everything for their children so much so that they hardly involve the child in anything. This is outright wrong and should be discouraged.

From organizing their school bag to putting the plate away after dinner, make sure your child is responsible for their work. Teach them these skills now, and there will be another helping hand at home.

151

### Teach them how to manage time.

Time is a resource that we cannot get back if we waste it. You can teach time management by getting your kid to claim responsibility for their own time. Begin by getting them an alarm clock that they can use to wake up on time for school, instead of you waking them up.

Also, you can purchase a planner for them to use to track their school work and other extra-curricular activities and also to keep track of what needs to be done and at what times. When they do this, they will habitually begin to allow definite amounts of time for play and work.

### Teach decision-making skills. T

he fact is that there are so many significant decisions we need to make throughout our lives. It is possible and advisable to instill decision-making skills in your child at an early age.

### Teach them money management and basic budgeting.

You can begin by giving your children a specific amount of pocket money every week or every two weeks that they have to use for their expenses. In the event where they desire to buy something a little more luxurious, you will instruct them to save up their pocket money to buy it.

Alternatively, you can lend them a hand by telling them that for every portion of the money they are able to save, you'll add a certain amount of money to their fund. This will provoke them into doing more.

The idea of reasonable shopping also comes under the concept of teaching your child about budgeting. Discuss with your child, telling them why you choose relatively cheaper options sometimes. When they want to buy a few things when you go shopping, buoy them up to pick one or two items if they're of the same kind. This kind of budgeting training grows a habit in your child to not waste money and to esteem its value.

Typically, children are introduced to the concept of money from the age of seven in school through subjects such as mathematics; however, nobody teaches them the importance of budgeting, planning, saving, and the real value of money as they have never handled money in real life.

In addition, you can open a bank account for your child, instructing them to make monthly cash deposits using money they get as gifts or as payments for services that they might render. This will instill the habit of saving and appreciating money.

### Teach how to shop.

It is important and advisable to always have your child accompany you when you go grocery shopping. Once your child identifies where the different categories of items are shelved, hand them a basket and tell them to get a few easy-to-find things for you.

Additionally, you can put your child in charge of buying a few things every month, such as snacks and juices. Also, remember to teach them how to pay for it while taking out time to model smart shopping yourself.

*Get them involved in simple cooking.*

You can teach your child how to make their peanut butter and jam sandwiches, how to butter a slice of bread, and how to make a salad. Also, you can have them tear up greens, squeeze lemons, and put chopped vegetables together to make a salad.

You can also get them to help you with baking, with handing you ingredients while you cook, or with keeping the kitchen table clean while you're preparing a meal.

The idea is for them to see you as a model and emulate you when they become independent. Your methods, cleanliness, and recipes might stay with them for years.

*Teach them the importance of environmental preservation.* Inculcating the significance of the environment and sustainability at an early age will show your child how to be more loving toward the planet. Teach your child why conserving the environment is important by making small lifestyle changes at home. Get them to practice eco-friendly habits in everything they do.

*Teach them to finish tasks independently.*
Insist that your children do their tasks. Allow them to pack their school bag, make their bed, and even pack their lunch. You can assist them in some of those chores, injecting some level of excitement into the exercise. Buy them new bedding and cushions themed around a cartoon or movie they love.

Have a sandwich station or a pancake station for breakfast with cut-up fruits, jams, syrup, spreads, and so on, so that they can make their plate and eat it the way they like.

1. *From the above chapter, what can you identify as the virtues lacking in your child/ward?*

_____

_____

_____

2. *What are some of the approaches you adopted in the quest to encourage your child to develop better life skills?*

_____

_____

_____

3. *Discuss with your child and pinpoint areas from the above chapter, which they still struggle to master.*

_____

_____

_____

# Chapter 13

## Life Skills Continued—Basic Life Skills to Equip Your Child With Continued

### A. Teach Them How To Interact with People

Considering the fact that every person we, as adults, are presently close to was a stranger to us at some point, it becomes illogical to teach our kids that every stranger is a danger to them. Alternatively, you can teach your children to do precisely what adults do— distinguishing between good strangers and bad strangers. Once you do this, you can then teach them how to interact with good strangers.

You should also teach them how to make friends, how to be friendly to good adults, and     just how they should go about interacting with these people. Since one of our most frequent tasks as adults is the interaction and management of people, then it makes it important to     teach our children how to effectively do the same. If we don't teach children this at a young     age, they may not develop positive social skills.

### B. Teach Them Cleaning and Other Household Chores

You can begin by simply asking your children to clean up their room, make their bed, and ensuring everything they own is properly placed. You can then go on to asking them to clean the dishes after having their meal. In addition, you can ask them to dust the living area, and then ask them to take the trash out; you can also ask them to set the table in whichever way they think looks the best and ask them to get creative with it.

You can ask them to join in on chores such as these to help you out or in exchange for their allowance. It's vital to practice these activities both in the context of an allowance and out of it. This will help your child learn to simply help out without being given anything in return.

## C.  Teach Them Basic Etiquettes

Teach your kid about appropriate behavior when at restaurants and how to place an order. Encourage them to place their orders and decide on what they want to eat on their own.

In addition, teach them how to eat with a knife and fork, how to place the knife and fork on the plate once they're done eating, and how to tip the waiters.

## D.  Teach Them How to Use Maps

In the event that you all are going somewhere, you can start by teaching your kids the routes around your house and test this by asking them to point out directions to your home or school the next time you're dropping them.

You can then ensure that your child learns how to read a map and also teach them how to use a GPS and follow its instructions.

### E.  Teach Them to Wash, Wash, Wash Your Clothes

You should get them involved in household chores such as doing the laundry. You can teach them how to operate the washing machine, what kind of clothes to wash separately, how much detergent to use, how to turn on the dryer, etc.

### F.  Teach Basics of Travelling

It is expected that your child knows traveling basics, aside from navigation. From learning to cycle to learning how to use public transportation, make sure your child knows how to do these things along with routes.

Additionally, teach them how to buy metro or bus tickets; teach them the basics of which metro train or bus goes to your house from school. These are vital skills that your child will need for later as well as for emergencies.

### G.  Teach Them to Embrace Diverse Perspectives in Situations

When your child comes to you about a difficulty that they had with their friend or a problem that they observed, encourage them to look at the situation that took place from the standpoint of others.

You can also explain the emotional responses of people at every chance you get. Explain why someone is sad or angry. This upsurges their problem-solving abilities and their level of understanding of the people around them greatly.

## H. Teach Them Resilience and Adaptability

Another essential skill would be to teach your child to be resilient. This can be done by making sure not to feed your child with solutions all the time. Equip your child to solve problems by themselves so that they're prepared to face trials as and when they come. They must learn resilience to become accustomed to diverse changes and different environments.

Make sure you have an open channel of communication to understand what your child is going through and help them out. Finally, you too must model resilient behavior at home.

Developing life skills is essential, so that our children have a passing idea of what they want to do in life and fundamentally keep in mind the kind of person they want to be.

By the time a child is six or seven years old, they've developed the footing of their temperament, and this kind of life skill development augments positive personality traits.

At this age, your child should be objectively independent in the way they function inside the house. They should also be following any safety rules that you lay down for them, which goes to show the personality trait of understanding and reasoning.

You can concentrate on educating your children in a manner that they find fun and entertaining so that you would have no worries when it comes to their morals and skills.

# Chapter 14

## Life Skills Continued—Life Skills Preschool Games

### A. Duck, Duck, Goose

| Category of activity | Game |
|---|---|
| Objective | This is an excellent game for teaching strategic thinking.<br><br>Duck, Duck, Goose teaches children to plan and gives them immediate feedback on the quality of their decisions. |
| Items to use | Play mat |

**How to play**

- Let all participating children sit in a circle.

- Let one child walk around the outside; the child should tap each head in turn, saying "duck."

- Finally, the child should pick one child to be the "goose." The child should then run around the circle, attempting to take that child's place before the "goose" catches them.

- If they reach the end without getting tagged, the "goose" returns to their seat, and the original player carries on around the circle.

- As children play this game more, they start to think about how to pick a "goose" who will give them a better chance of getting back to their seats without getting tagged.

Take note of the various responses of the child at each stage and with each instruction.

Important notes:

_____

_____

_____

_____

_____

_____

_____

_____

## B. Musical Chairs

| Category of activity | Game |
|---|---|
| Objective | This game teaches kids to deal with arguments peacefully, handle disappointments, and practice patience. They must also learn to use their words to work out quarrels about whose chair is whose or who got there "first." |
| Items to use | Chairs |

**How to play**

- Set chairs in a circle—one fewer than the number of kids in the game.

- Play music, as kids walks around the circle.

- Every time the music stops, children must try to sit on a chair.

- Children who don't get a chair are out.

- Then remove a chair and begin again.

- As the game of musical chairs advances, children must learn to handle the frustration of being out of the game, consequently practicing patience and waiting graciously.

- Be sure to have an adult on hand precisely to make sure skirmishes are settled calmly and to help kids who are no longer in the game stay happy.

Take note of the various responses of the child at each stage and with each instruction.

Important notes:

_____

_____

_____

_____

_____

_____

_____

_____

_____

## C. Simon Says

| Category of activity | Game |
|---|---|
| Objective | Simon Says is an excellent game for helping kids learn to pay close attention to instructions, while also giving them a taste of leadership. |
| Items to use | Play mat |

## How to play

- One kid asks their peers to do silly actions by saying, *"Simon says, tap your head"* or *"Simon Says, jump like monkeys,"* for instance.

- Then the other kids will do the action, but only as long as the leader adds "Simon says" to their instructions.

- Kids who don't pay attention would realize that if they don't listen, they'll be the only ones doing the silly action. That gives them extra inspiration to listen carefully to the entire set of commands before getting started.

**Take note of the various responses of the child at each stage and with each instruction.**

**Important notes:**

_____

_____

_____

_____

_____

_____

_____

_____

# D. Row Your Boat

| Category of activity | Game |
|---|---|
| Objective | Self-awareness is an essential skill for children to develop as part of the learning process. When children are small, this can start with *physical* self-awareness. Knowing how to moderate one's body is a very valuable skill that arranges kids for later life. It also helps children focus on auditory cues and match their physical movements to them. |
| Items to use | Play mat |

**How to play**

- Pair children up facing one another with knees bent up in front of them and holding hands.

- Instruct them to rock back and forth in time to the song "Row, Row, Row Your Boat." They'll need to work together and keep an eye on their movements at all times.

- It works best to play this game with a CD or a song on YouTube, so you can incorporate a "freeze" element by stopping music abruptly.

Take note of the various responses of the child at each stage and with each instruction.

Important notes:

_____

_____

_____

_____

_____

_____

_____

_____

_____

# E. Hide and Seek

| Category of activity | Game |
| --- | --- |
| Objective | Hide and Seek is a great game for teaching problem-solving. In order to stay hidden for the longest possible time, children have to evaluate their options, so that they can pick the best possible hiding spot.<br><br>This builds spatial awareness because kids must contemplate factors such as which hiding places will offer the most cover from the most vantage points.<br><br>As they gain experience with the game, kids will take an even more in-depth valuation approach, thinking about which spots are frequently used during free play and therefore most likely to be checked first. |
| Items to use | None |

Take note of the various responses of the child at each stage and with each instruction.

Important notes:

_____

_____

_____

_____

_____

_____

_____

_____

## F. Parachute Game

| Category of activity | Game |
|---|---|
| Objective | Playing with a parachute is a fun way for kids to learn teamwork. |
| Items to use | Play mat |

**How to play**

- Kids stand around a circle, holding a parachute (or large sheet) between them.

- When a ball or other object is placed on the parachute, kids toss the ball up and down.

- Kids must move in sync, or the ball will fall off the side of the parachute.

- If playing with a big parachute, kids have to work together to keep multiple balls in play at the same time or learn how to throw the parachute up so that one child can run underneath before the parachute falls.

**Take note of the various responses of the child at each stage and with each instruction.**

**Important notes:**

_____

_____

_____

_____

_____

_____

_____

_____

# G. Hopscotch

| Category of activity | Game |
|---|---|
| Objective | This classic sidewalk game is perfect for developing critical thinking skills.<br><br>Since it's often difficult to avoid the square with the rock while hopping on one foot, kids will need to plan to find the best "route" through the course. |
| Items to use | Play mat |

**How to play**

- Kids draw the hopscotch shape on the sidewalk.

- They then take turns tossing a rock underhand at the hopscotch shape.

- They then must navigate the hopscotch course while avoiding the square the rock landed on.

> Take note of the various responses of the child at each stage and with each instruction.

> Important notes:
>
> _____
>
> _____
>
> _____
>
> _____
>
> _____
>
> _____
>
> _____
>
> _____

## H. Red Light, Green Light

| Category of activity | Game |
|---|---|
| Objective | Red Light, Green Light is great for teaching patience. After all, children don't love to stand still. |
| | To win at Red Light, Green Light, kids need to rein in their impulse to run forward and instead choosing a pace where they can stop instantly if the leader starts to turn. As they near the leader, they'll also have to learn how to wait for the exact right moment to rush forward. If they misjudge and go too soon, they'll have to start over from the beginning. |
| Items to use | None |

## How to play

- To play, one kid stands facing away at the other side of the field.

- The goal is to be the first to touch that person without getting caught moving.

- When the person is facing away, that's a green light, and kids can move toward them. When the leader turns around to face the group, that's a red light, and kids must stop moving.

- Anyone that the leader catches still in motion has to go back to the starting line.

| Take note of the various responses of the child at each stage and with each instruction. |
|---|
| **Important notes:** |
| _____ |
| _____ |
| _____ |
| _____ |
| _____ |
| _____ |
| _____ |
| _____ |

## I.  Sleeping Lions

| Category of activity | Game |
| --- | --- |
| Objective | It's important for kids to learn how to stay focused despite distractions. Sleeping Lions is a fun way for kids to learn this important life skill.<br><br>Sleeping Lions encourages kids to be silly, as they try to wake up their peers.<br><br>That's extremely hard for young children to do, and the focusing skills they practice during Sleeping Lions will help a child later on when they're trying to learn in boisterous environments. |
| Items to use | None |

**How to play**

- During this preschool game, all the children lie down and pretend to be asleep.

- To stay "asleep," kids have to keep themselves focused on not moving a muscle—no matter how much their peers try to distract them.

- Then one person walks among the group (without touching anyone, trying to convince kids into reacting and opening their eyes).

- The last kid to still look like they're "sleeping" is the winner.

Take note of the various responses of the child at each stage and with each instruction.

Important notes:

_____

_____

_____

_____

_____

_____

_____

_____

# Chapter 15

## Life Skills Continued—Life Skills Preschool Games Continued

### A. Balloon Bop

| Category of activity | Game |
|---|---|
| Objective | This simple game can be so much fun for toddlers. It's easy for them to succeed, and they will love how easily they can maneuver these lightweight objects.<br><br>Not only is it a rainy day boredom buster but it's also great for hand-eye coordination and motor development. |
| Items to use | Balloon |

**How to play**

- Blow up several balloons for your child.

- Help them to throw the balloons into the air as high as they can to try and reach the furthest point possible.

- If your child is a little older, tie the string up high, and see if they can aim the balloon to go over the string.

- Encourage them to try to catch the balloon on their return back toward the ground.

**Take note of the various responses of the child at each stage and with each instruction.**

**Important notes:**

_____

_____

_____

_____

_____

_____

_____

_____

## B. Indoor Cubby House

| Category of activity | Game |
|---|---|
| Objective | This is yet another great activity for indoor play (especially if it is raining). It's simple to create a play space for the kids and allows your child to dream up many different possibilities.<br><br>The cubby house could be a house, a rocket ship, a teddy bear hospital, or even a shop. This game will encourage play, social skills, and imagination development. |
| Items to use | Blankets<br><br>Pegs<br><br>Cushions |

**How to play**

- Use the blankets and bedspread to make a cubby house. You can cover dining chairs set out into a square or rectangular area, a dining table with the blankets laid on top, or the backs of lounge room sofas.

- Use the pegs to secure the blankets in place.

- Bring cushions or blankets into the cubby house to make it comfortable.

**Take note of the various responses of the child at each stage and with each instruction.**

**Important notes:**

_____

_____

_____

_____

_____

_____

_____

_____

## C. Bubbles

| Category of activity | Game |
|---|---|
| Objective | No matter what your age, bubbles will always make you happy and smile. But they are not just for fun! Bubbles can give kids a lot of help in developing essential skills such as visual tracking skills (to track and see where the bubbles go), sensory processing skills (bubbles are wet, sticky, large and small, and learning to blow the bubbles can help the child to learn to focus on the act itself), and social skills (asking an adult to blow more bubbles and sharing equipment with other children). |
| Items to use | Bubble mixture (but dishwashing liquid and water also works perfectly if you run out)<br><br>A device to create the bubbles. You can find these at any good toy store, but you may have an item in the home that will work just as well. Think of any kitchen utensils you may have such as cookie cutters. Or if you're chasing bigger bubbles, use an old wire coat hanger shaped into a circle. |

## How to play

- Dip the bubble maker into the solution.

- Blow the bubbles through and watch, as your child enjoys the sight of bubbles.

Take note of the various responses of the child at each stage and with each instruction.

Important notes:

_____

_____

_____

_____

_____

_____

_____

_____

_____

## D. Walk the Plank

| Category of activity | Game |
|---|---|
| Objective | This activity is great for developing balance and enhancing gross motor development skills. If walking barefoot, it's also a great way to improve sensory processing, as the texture of the wood will be different from the grass. |
| Items to use | A flat piece of wood at least 5 centimeters thick and 2 meters long. If you don't have one this long, a shorter piece will do.<br><br>Optional: a piece of blue material and black cardboard to make fin shapes for extra effect. |

**How to play**

- Lay the wood on the grass/material.

- Show your toddler or child how to walk on the plank with your arms out to each side.

- To extend the activity, feel free to add towels under the plank to raise it off of the ground or walk sideways along the plank. Walking barefoot (so long as there are no splinters in the wood) is also an option.

**Take note of the various responses of the child at each stage and with each instruction.**

**Important notes:**

_____

_____

_____

_____

_____

_____

_____

_____

_____

# E. Ball Rolling Exercise

| Category of activity | Game |
|---|---|
| Objective | Having these simple rules will teach a child language skills, as they understand what is taught to them. The physical motion of rolling the ball also works on their gross motor skills and, depending on the ball, the texture will also improve their sensory processing skills. This activity is great for those who cannot kick a ball yet or are weak on their feet, as this can all be done while sitting. |
| Items to use | A ball |

**How to play**

- Sit a meter or two away from your child on the ground, facing each other.

- Roll the ball toward each other.

- If the ball touches the other person's legs, the person who rolled the ball scores a point.

Take note of the various responses of the child at each stage and with each instruction.

Important notes:

_____

_____

_____

_____

_____

_____

_____

_____

## F. Animal Friends

| Category of activity | Game |
|---|---|
| Objective | Developing coordination and balance as children imitate their favorite animals is one of the key outcomes of this activity. Play and social skills are also developed as well as phonological (sound) awareness and articulation skills. |
| Items to use | None |

**How to play**

- Whether it is indoors or outdoors, select different animals to imitate.

- Choose animals that have obvious features, such as an elephant and its long trunk or a bird, and flap your arms like wings.

- Ask your child to pick an animal for you both to reenact.

- Alternatively, you can act like an animal and ask the child to guess which animal you are and vice-versa.

---

Take note of the various responses of the child at each stage and with each instruction.

Important notes:

_____

_____

_____

_____

_____

_____

_____

_____

## G. Do you Hear What I Hear?

| Category of activity | Game |
|---|---|
| Objective | This exercise is great for improving sound awareness and articulation. Language skills are worked on by asking the child how they think their ears and eyes work, and to get them to start thinking about the way their bodies work. The sounds they listen to and learning to differentiate between sounds helps them to understand their world even more. |
| Items to use | Markers<br><br>Whiteboard |

**How to play**

- Draw a picture of an open eye on the left and a closed eye on the right of the board.

- Ask your child to list the sounds they can hear with their eyes open. List these things under the picture of the open eye.

- Then ask them to close their eyes. Ask them to sit and listen for a minute or two.

- Ask them to list the things they can hear with their eyes closed.

- Ask them why they think they can hear different sounds when their eyes are closed.

Take note of the various responses of the child at each stage and with each instruction.

Important notes:

_____

_____

_____

_____

_____

_____

_____

_____

## H. Polka Dot Flowers

| Category of activity | Game |
|---|---|
| Objective | Fine motor skills are encouraged to develop in this activity, as your toddler learns to use primarily one hand. Their sensory processing skills are also worked on by establishing different colored dyes and demonstrating how the dye reacts on the water and the paper. It's both fun and helps them to be more creative. |
| Items to use | Plastic eyedroppers<br><br>Colored food dye<br><br>Small containers of water<br><br>Cupcake paper cases or coffee filters |

**How to play**

- Have the child use the eyedropper to add colored dye to the water.

- Encourage them to practice squeezing the dye into and out of the eyedropper.

- Once they understand how to use the eyedropper, ask them to use the dropper to add drops of colored water to the cupcake paper cases or coffee filters to make patterns or flowers.

Take note of the various responses of the child at each stage and with each instruction.

Important notes:

_____

_____

_____

_____

_____

_____

_____

_____

## I. Clap a Name

| Category of activity | Game |
|---|---|
| Objective | This activity is perfect for working on your child's' phonological awareness and social skills. Their articulation and language skills will also improve, and this activity will help them to understand English a lot better. The clapping in this exercise also helps to develop fine motor skills. |
| Items to use | None |

189

## How to play

- Explain how syllables work in words. So as an example, explain that "cat" has one syllable, whereas the word "elephant" has three.

- Clap to each word's syllables. So for "cat," you clap your hands with the word. With "elephant," you clap at each syllable like "el-e-phant."

- Ask your child to think of new words to use for the activity.

- Clap along with them to the syllables of the words.

- Even ask them to show you how many syllables are there in their name and their friends' names.

---

**Take note of the various responses of the child at each stage and with each instruction.**

**Important notes:**

_____

_____

_____

_____

_____

_____

_____

_____

## A. Touchy-Feely Box

| Category of activity | Game |
|---|---|
| Objective | Exploring the world around them is a great part of growing up and developing. This activity encourages children to discover items and learn how to describe them accurately. Sensory processing, social skills, fine motor skills, and speech skills are all encouraged within this activity, making it both educational and fun for kids. |
| Items to use | Shoebox with holes cut out of each end<br><br>Two shells<br><br>Two pinecones<br><br>Two rocks |

**How to play**

- Place the items into the box, and place the lid on.

- Have the child sit on one side of the box and a friend (or yourself) sit on the other side of the box.

- Have one child grab an item and try to describe to the other child what they are holding.

- The other child needs to use their descriptions to find the same item.

- When they think they've found it, remove the lid to see if the items are the same.

- Ask them to use words like "bumpy," "smooth," "rough," etc.

- Have the children take turns to describe the items.

---

**Take note of the various responses of the child at each stage and with each instruction.**

**Important notes:**

_____

_____

_____

_____

_____

_____

_____

_____

## Get the Letter of Intent for Free

Building a relationship with our readers is the very best thing about writing. We occasionally send newsletters with details on new releases, special offers, and other bits of news relating to autism and special needs.

And if you sign up to the mailing list, we'll send you the Letter of Intent E-book, which is worth $35.00, for free. You can get Letter of Intent, for free, by signing up at https://diffnotless.com/

### *About the Letter of Intent E-book:*

No one else knows your child as well as you do, and no one ever could. You are a walking encyclopedia of your child's history, experiences, habits, and wishes. If your child has special needs, the family's history adds a helpful chapter to your child's book, one detailing his unique medical, behavioral, and educational requirements.

A letter of intent helps your loved ones and your child manage a difficult transition when you no longer are the primary caregiver. A letter of intent is an important planning tool for parents of children with special needs (including adult children), and also guides your child's future caregivers in making the most appropriate life decisions for your child, including providing direction to your child's trustee in fulfilling his or her fiduciary responsibilities.

The letter of intent may be addressed to anyone you wish.

This document addresses the following points:

- emotional information,

- future vision for the child,

- biographical and personal information,

- medical information,

- personality traits and preferences,

- habits and hygiene,

- meals and dietary requirements, and

- much more.

Once you prepare, sign, and date the letter of intent, you should review the document annually and update it as necessary. It is important that you let your child's potential future caregiver know that the letter of intent exists and where it can be accessed; even better, you can review the document with the caregiver on an annual basis. The letter of intent should be placed with all of your other relevant legal and personal documents concerning your child.

## Found This Book Useful? You Can Make a Big Difference

Reviews are the most powerful tools in our arsenal when it comes to getting attention for our books. Much as we'd like to, we don't have the financial muscle of a New York publisher. We can't take out full page ads in the newspaper or put posters on the subway.

But we do have something much more powerful and effective than that, and it's something that those publishers would kill to get their hands on.

A committed and loyal bunch of readers like you.

Honest reviews of our books help bring them to the attention of other readers.

If you've found this book useful, we would be very grateful if you could spend just five minutes leaving a review (it can be as short as you like) on the book's Amazon page.

Thank you very much.

## Other Books by Susan Jules

Have you read them all?

What will happen to my Special Needs Child when I am gone: A Detailed Guide to Secure Your Child's Emotional and Financial Future— https://geni.us/At0afS

Let's Talk: A Conversational Skills Workbook for Children with Autism & Special Needs—https://geni.us/dnll

105 Activities for Your Child with Autism and Special Needs: Enable them to Thrive, Interact, Develop and Play— https://geni.us/tSu9

Made in the USA
Middletown, DE
10 August 2021